Ethical Marketing and the New Consumer

Ethical Marketing and the New Consumer

Chris Arnold

WILEY

A John Wiley and Sons, Ltd., Publication

This edition first published 2009
© 2009 John Wiley & Sons, Ltd

Registered office
John Wiley & Sons Ltd, The Atrium, Southern Gate, Chichester, West Sussex,
PO19 8SQ, United Kingdom

For details of our global editorial offices, for customer services and for
information about how to apply for permission to reuse the copyright material
in this book please see our website at www.wiley.com.

Library of Congress Cataloging-in-Publication Data

Arnold, Chris.
   Ethical marketing and the new consumer / Chris Arnold.
      p.   cm.
   Includes bibliographical references and index.
   ISBN 978-0-470-74302-7 (cloth)
   1. Marketing—Moral and ethical aspects.   2. New Age consumer.   I. Title.
   HF5415.A743 2009
   658.8—dc22

                                                          2009021630

A catalogue record for this book is available from the British Library.

ISBN 978-0-470-74302-7

Set in 11/13 pt ITC Garamond Light by SNP Best-set Typesetter Ltd., Hong Kong
Printed in Great Britain by TJ International Ltd, Padstow, Cornwall

CONTENTS

FOREWORD

Ethics. In our purchases, in our business, in our lives.

Any conversation on this topic is likely to be a lively one. Because your ethic will be different to mine and to the next person we meet. Ethics are personal and to my mind stem from self awareness. When you truly consider the effects of your actions, whether that's how you travel or perhaps the food you choose, you begin to develop and understand your own moral code. Sounds simple? Well probably not. Already we're in a minefield of doubt and confusion.

What are the boundaries of your ethical behaviour? For you is it about environment, politics, our fellow man, or the animals? Quickly we see that the more we think, the more there is to think about! When you start asking questions you are taken deeper into your subject.

How can you determine the whole story of much of the 'stuff' that you have around you? Much that we have around us that is produced by big business is no longer the product of a single source; little is produced in one country let alone one factory. As a consequence our trust in big brands becomes ever more important, and yet more difficult.

If local sourcing feels right, what happens when you consider the potential effect to communities abroad that have developed over the last few years to bring us the things we have come to expect on the shelves in the shops around us? How recently were green beans seasonal? And baby corn on the cob a luxury few of us would contemplate? Eschewing these may seem an ethical choice, but the consequences down the line may leave us less comfortable.

In business ethics starts a bit further back, with ethos. What does the company believe? How prepared is it to tell the whole truth? And can it deliver to its shareholders while remaining true to the ethos.

Starting a business in a 'good' way is a great foundation for your future. Remaining true to your beliefs is a challenge, but it's easier than changing them. You'll have many pitfalls to watch out for, and you'll spend more time deciding on each supplier. But do consider too that just by staying true you are already moving others in the right direction – with every question you ask you help another business to question itself.

Moving a business' ethos is probably the greatest challenge in doing the right thing. I'm delighted every time a huge business makes a genuine change for the better – but woe betide those who spin a story! There are now so many green watchers waiting to leap on every false claim, or even ones that aren't supported elsewhere in the business.

Improving a business' ethos is a massive challenge, but one that brings rewards to so many of those measures we watch so keenly such as ability to recruit and retain talent, customer satisfaction, trust, and the vital area of customer retention.

Once someone has made a conscious shift to a better product as a consequence of their heightened awareness of the effects of that purchase how hard will it be to then switch that conscience off and return to just buying on price?

For some the word 'marketing' seems unethical, after all, it's the driving force behind churn and this instant, disposable society we live in. Those that have mixed their politics with their ethics see marketing as a bad capitalist tool. Yet where would charities be without marketing? Red Nose Day is a marketing event for Comic Relief, and despite the recession, it has had one of its best years this year.

New ethical products have to compete with traditional ones in a highly competitive marketplace. Often marginally more expensive they have to sell themselves hard, conveying the added value they bring. With less spend and little distribution, it is good marketing that can give them the advantage, win business and help build a strong customer base. With that comes all the benefits of the support they pass down the line.

Even those ethical brands that don't seem to employ high profile marketing techniques like TV adverts are employing many other subtler marketing techniques. Without them most would quickly fade away.

For those brands that have adopted more ethical values it's often simply about communications. Telling people the story in a compelling way.

Love it or hate it, you can't turn your back on marketing. It's an essential tool to growing a business. But like any tool it requires expert use. Use it badly and it can do more damage than good. Use it well and you will reap success.

Kelvin Collins
Former Head of Brand Management
Co-operative Financial Services
www.kelvincollins.com

I
INTRODUCTION

Although green issues have been with us for several decades it's only recently that brands have started to take them seriously. But rather than exercise carefully considered marketing many have jumped on the green bandwagon. Now millions of dollars and pounds of marketing spend are being spent on campaigns to make brands look more ethical, sadly most are a waste of money. Phrases like 'green-wash' and 'ethicalwash' are an apt way to describe most marketing activity. There seems to be little communication between CSR (Corporate Social Responsibility) and marketing departments and little understanding of consumer attitudes. Call it lazy, ignorant, poorly advised or just that too many brands have fallen into a process of just churning ads out – and green is just another brief – but there really isn't much good eco-ethical marketing about.

On one level this book should help marketing and brand managers avoid becoming a victim of greenwash or worse, damaging the reputation of their brand. For eco-ethical businesses it will provide useful marketing guidance. And for students, it will offer some challenging ideas.

This book seeks to explore new ideas, provide a better understanding of the eco-ethical or 'new' consumer and turn a few ideas upside down and even inside out. There are already a few myths that need exploding and as for any rules which you've been told, ignore them. One thing you'll discover is that maybe green isn't the best way forward if you want to be seen as an ethical brand. When we started the People versus Planet debate we challenged a lot of people to think about people messages against environmental ones. The outcome of our research was both illuminating and surprising to many.

The book will also show you how using traditional advertising techniques may be less effective than you thought. Or that you probably need to start with a different strategy than the one you first thought if you want to communicate the ethical values of a brand.

Advertising and marketing are not a science and there are no rules, just learning. It's an area full of well argued opinions and debate and as soon as someone thinks they have discovered a rule everything changes. I always compare it to music and fashion, what's in one year is out the next. The consumer is constantly changing and we've seen a dramatic change over the last few years. Combined with a recession, the world of marketing is being shaken up.

This book isn't a rule book, a guide maybe but more than anything it's been written to get you thinking, to challenge conventional ideas and explore new areas. When people ask me what I do for a living I say I make people think and help them solve problems, hopefully this book will do exactly that. Marketing is an adventure, a journey of the unexplored, which is why it's such an exciting area to work in. But the moment it becomes a process it's usually not good marketing. Think of any great campaign and great marketing idea and almost all of them broke with tradition. New ideas equal new opportunities. But this also requires people to be brave, 'there's no success in the comfort zone' was a quote from of one very successful entrepreneur I know. Another entrepreneur who I worked with, Simon Woodroffe (Yo!) said, 'If you follow conventional thinking, all you'll ever be is conventional'. Worse, and this is my addition, you could be out of business.

One key thing that I've learnt over the years is that too many brands start in the wrong place. They make assumptions, base decisions on wrong information and then write briefs that end up sending everyone in the wrong direction. The tools that you'll find in this book such the R&E Line, the

Ethical Sphere and a few other ideas will provide you with very powerful weapons to improve your marketing. There are sections that will help give you a greater insight into consumers. We haven't filled the book with case studies, but we are inviting any business to submit their own case studies on the website http://www.ecoethicalmarketing. info. There will also be room for discussion and debate, and in this area there's a lot of it. In time we hope that it will become a hub of ideas and information for brands, students and small businesses working within the eco-ethical arena.

THE STRUCTURE

When Wiley first asked me to write this book (and it took longer than planned with so much material), as a creative marketing consultant I asked a few questions about readers, distribution and statistics about reading.

One fact that was hardly surprising is that a large per-centage of business books that are bought are never read properly. Of those books that are read few are read cover to cover, most are dipped in and out of. How many of us have shelves of books that we mean to read one day? Many of which have travelled thousands of miles in our hand luggage without ever being opened?

To 'eat the elephant whole' is something most of us don't do, we live in an age of bite size media, in a world where we seek out information in fast to digest forms. Time is one thing few of us have to spare. We no longer think in a linear way but within a chaotic 'fuzzy' world. Thanks to the internet to start at the beginning and end at the end is now a very outdated idea. We like to drop in and drop out, zig zag about, gathering up those nuggets of relevant information as we go along. Time is too short and precious a commodity to waste on waffle or irrelevance. A hundred words of insight or vision are worth more than 10 000 words of rubbish. We are all in search of knowledge and leadership.

Rather than write a book that linked one chapter to another this book is designed to be read in any order, you decide. There is a structure but there is no reason to start at the beginning and read to the end. It's not really a unique or original model, many education books are written this way, as are magazines.

THANKS

There are many people who have helped in putting this book together, too many to list – they know who they are. My apologies to those whose case studies, interviews, brands or thoughts have not been included – we had to cut over 20% of the original manuscript. But we have launched a website where case studies and deleted chapters will be posted (see the final chapter). However, my greatest thanks go to Sarah Eden, an eco-writer who has helped with research, processing a great deal of information and doing the first edit. A green star if there ever was one.

2
THE POWER OF
BRAND ETHOS

FROM ETHICS TO ETHOS MARKETING

We talk about 'ethical marketing' but perhaps we should adopt a more progressive term, 'ethos marketing'. This makes a brand feel less marginal, and after all, shouldn't all marketing be ethical?

Ethos is probably one of the most important things a brand (and therefore a business) has. Yet so few bother to market it. Worse, many businesses have lost it, turning into bland brands with few, if any, values.

The mistake many brands make is when it comes to a makeover. Things are tough and the board needs the company to reinvent itself so they decide they need a new corporate identity. 'We need a rebrand'. What they get is a new look, not a new brand. A brand isn't defined by its logo but by what it does. What it does is defined by its ethos, which gives it the why. It really is that simple.

Brands are like people and no matter what clothes you wear others will see you for what you are through your behaviour. I once worked with a manager whose only value was how much things cost and whether he could cut it. He did everything on the cheap, not surprisingly quality or ethics were not part of his agenda. How many companies behave in the same way? The public can soon spot a company that cares only about money, which means it won't care about quality, people or ethics. 'A principle isn't a principle unless it costs you something'. And in the business of ethics, you often have to sacrifice some margin for values.

WHY REPUTATION IS MORE IMPORTANT THAN LOGOS

The other great mistake companies make is to think brand. People talk about reputation. So does the City. Reputation is what others say about you, it reflects your true values.

Innocent is a prime example of a brand that has grown off a strong ethos and reputation. Every touching point with the brand is defined by its ethos. If you meet their marketing team at a show they are friendly, energetic and honest. It's all about quality. The ingredients and the people are the best. You can tell the company cares about what is put into its bottle and who puts it in.

You can't say the same for any other soft drink. Brands like Coke have suffered so much adverse publicity, especially over the water scandal in India, that its behaviour has redefined the brand. Even given billions of dollars of advertising, kids see it as a bad brand.

Ethos is what defines the why and what we do. I always say that if your company has a strong ethos then you should be able to send any member of staff out to buy coffee cups and they'll know exactly what to buy. I heard a story about a very dynamic digital company who sent their PA out to get napkins. She returned with Christmas themed ones, and this was in July. Her explanation was that it felt like Christmas every day in the office. That's one hell of a great ethos to have.

NO ETHOS

But when it comes to no ethos, the classic was Woolworth's. When I first started my career in advertising at McCann-Erickson in London it was the first account I worked on. It wasn't much fun and the client played so safe. Even then, over 20 years ago, it was in trouble. The store had become too diverse and no one knew what it really stood for. Twenty years on the same problem has led to its failure in the UK. Even ordinary consumers have used the phrase 'Woolworth's, what do they stand for these days?'

The original store started in 1878 in America and was a five & dime store, the original £1 shop. In the beginning its purpose was simple – bring great value and choice to the customer. Having grown to one of the world's largest retail brands in the world, it started to decline in the 1980s. In the US it diversified into sportswear by way of the Foot Locker brand, with the last Woolworth's closing in 1997.

It first opened in the UK in 1909 in Liverpool, growing to over 800 stores with almost 90% of the general public making at least one visit a year. But now everyone was bringing great value to the customer and you needed a new angle. Woolworth's tried numerous routes but a failure to define its ethos and values, and therefore its brand, is one of the reasons it failed. I noticed recently that there wasn't one product in the store that championed any aspect of ethics. Just how far can you have your finger off the pulse? It seems that the real 'wonder of Woollies' (as the ad slogan used to go) was how it managed to survive for so long.

BECOMING RICHER THROUGH ETHICS

Ethos is one of the most powerful things a business can tap into, yet I've rarely heard any corporate identity design company mention the word. The trouble with ethos is that it's hard to fake or to demand that people adopt it, if your behaviour as a business is in conflict. Worse is when a business, like Body Shop, is built on a strong ethical ethos and then the money men move in and ethics is replaced with greed.

When Body Shop was sold to L'Oréal in 2006 there was a massive clash of ethos. Body Shop under Anita Roddick had a strong policy of not testing on animals. By contrast, L'Oréal had tested on animals (though they claimed they hadn't done so since 1989, but these things stick to a brand, as Nestlé knows all too well when it comes to baby milk). Customers were outraged. There were even boycotts. Many thought Roddick had sold out. She was after all the driving force behind the company and her ethos was the brand's. L'Oréal also represented the type of company driven by profits and this again jarred with the public's view of The Body Shop, even though it was financially very successful with over 2000 shops in over 50 countries and a sale value of over £650 million – who says you can't make money from ethics?

The combination of a strong ethos and a strong personality is one of the most powerful things you can take to market. It connects on every level with the public. Even a grey brand like M&S found new life in Plan A, not just because it's a great piece of marketing but because it was delivered via the head of the company. Somehow, one believed that Plan A was as much Stuart Rose's vision as the company's. We trust people not corporations and when people speak we listen and want to believe. So many ethical brands are started by passionate individuals whose values are those of their brand, so it's not surprising that we trust them more than large corporate ones.

LOOKING IN THE MIRROR

My advice to any business is to look at yourself first before you start to waste a fortune on marketing. Get your ethos right. Do you even have one? If not then you need to develop one. Ask all your staff, suppliers and customers what they think your values and ethos are. What drives the business? What is the spirit of it? You could be in for a shock.

Now ask, are we communicating this? Chances are, you aren't. Instead you've drifted off into product advantage or highlighting some rare bean you've discovered on a field trip to the rainforest. That's all well and good but make sure you also tell people the why. Why you picked it. Why you would rather buy it from a tribe in Bolivia than a chemist in Romford. Why you think it's important. Values soon come through. And when the customer knows the why behind what you do, that it is a good and ethical one, they trust you. And without trust, few brands can survive.

Your ethos can also be a platform to grow from. A company that sells organic fair trade nuts can do other things. It can champion causes, challenge the bad boys or seek to use its influence (and customers) to make change in society. Body Shop and Lush have sometimes acted more like Greenpeace than retailers. Benetton made us think about ethical diversity while shopping for clothes. These actions may seem frivolous to narrow minded accountants but they bring depth to a brand, and actions do speak louder than words. This is the new spirit of the age which some people talk about in business. An extra dimension to marketing the old school can't see; the third dimension. Or better, the ethical dimension.

Actions create experience and experience is far more influential than words or pictures. Innocent grew its business on actions and ethos, not through a million dollar ad campaign, all that came well after they were established.

SUMMARY

Almost all business start-ups begin with an ethos. But somewhere along the road to becoming big it fades. Suddenly a company doesn't know why it does what it does or what its values are. All it knows is that the shareholders want more every quarter. So many big brands have no ethos. Consumers tune into an ethos and it's far more powerful than any ad because if you know the 'why' you know 'how' they will behave. And what you do, not what you say, defines your brand reputation. And no matter what you think, it's very hard to undo a bad reputation.

3
ETHICAL – REALITY OR A BRAND IMAGE?

WHEN IS AN ETHICAL REPUTATION NOT THE SAME AS BEING ETHICAL?

If you ask the public which brands are ethical and which aren't you get a fairly consistent point of view. The Ethical Brand Index, created by Karen Fraser, is the most accurate measure of brand perception in relationship to ethics. Like similar surveys, top of the list are the predictable brands – The Body Shop, Green & Black, Innocent, Co-op, etc. Bottom of the list are fast foods and fuels. No surprises there. But is perception the same as reality?

One brand regarded highly for its ethics is Pret a Manger, founded in 1986 by Sinclair Beecham and Julian Metcalfe. It is a stylish sandwich chain with a passion for food that boasts, 'Pret creates handmade natural food avoiding the obscure chemicals, additives and preservatives common to so much of the "prepared" and "fast" food on the market today'. This may be true but what about other ethical issues such as health? Let's consider the ethics of calories. Their crisps are calorific and many of their sandwiches are loaded with mayonnaise. A criticism of fast food is its high calorie content but many sandwiches are the same, if not higher in calories than a hamburger.

Pret's design and marketing is up there with Starbucks; clean looking, modern and fresh, with stunning graphics and entertaining slogans. As we all feel positive towards Pret we don't think or want to criticize them. I am a great fan of their food but I know if I'm on a diet it's not always the best place to go.

I really doubt whether most customers could recite the claims of Pret but the lasting impression and experience is so positive that the consumer sees them as ethical. Why is that? I doubt the same would be said of Subway (which makes one of the most calorific 'subs' you can buy).

By contrast, Subway looks cheap and low quality. Poor graphics, shop fitting and presentation, it's not premium in any way. How does that make us feel towards them? Hardly positive.

The big difference is ethos. Subway has none, Pret has buckets of it. It feels like it has a passion for food, whereas Subway feels like a fast food franchise.

THE UNTAPPED POWER OF ETHOS

Brands that come top of many surveys live and breathe some form of ethics. They deliver it from the heart. Ethos is a key element to looking and feeling ethical. You can't fake it, people see through false claims. And ethos starts with people. We trust people; we don't trust big corporations or faceless franchises. The reason M&S's Plan A was so convincing was that it was delivered by a person – Stuart Rose – not via a corporate mouthpiece.

If you want the consumer to feel good about you and view you as ethical you need to dig out your ethos and deliver it.

So what about those at the bottom of ethical surveys? Is McDonald's really the evil monster it's made out to be? There's a problem here, if it's so bad why do so many people eat there? Why do so many parents have their kid's birthday party there and why, in a recession, do their sales go up? Why do people queue to work there?

Let's consider some of the criticisms. Cows are bad for the planet and McDonald's means lots of cows. This is the left wing vegetarian argument based upon cows being producers of methane, which is bad. True, but all animals produce methane. Rotting vegetables produce gases as well. On the other hand, isn't it just crap food that's bad for us. Yep, eating a hamburger a day may be bad but so are some sandwiches from Boots, M&S or Pret; or a curry, a Chinese take-a-way, pizza and fish & chips and a million other things. All these are high in calories too but no one is attacking them especially as unethical.

What about energy companies? Shell, Exxon, BP and the rest get a bad press. When Shell created its flowers ad based on the fact it was using some of its waste CO_2 to grow flowers (even though it was less than 0.4%) it was heavily criticised by many people, including the Advertising Standards Authority (ASA). As advertising goes the ad was a good one but it failed to understand the ethical market. A touch more honesty and maybe some intent, 'we aim to use more CO_2 year on year for good purposes ...' would have raised it above criticism. But presented the way it was placed it in prime greenwash territory. Ironically, it was no greater exaggeration than many ads but it was an oil company trying to look green and to some this is unthinkable and any attempt to look green must be shot down.

The bad news for environmentalists is that the oil companies are putting millions into good causes and alternative energy projects. The problem for oil companies is that they don't know how to get that across in a way which is convincing (traditional ad agencies still don't understand it).

The point is: there's little sense or reason, as to who or what the public thinks are or are not ethical. It's in the unpredictable nature of consumers to arrive at their own distorted ideas. Fish & Chips and beer is good, McDonald's is bad. As Tears for Fears put it, it's a mad, mad world.

IT'S NOT HOW MUCH YOU MAKE BUT HOW YOU MAKE IT

Consumers are not fond of companies that just make money. They don't begrudge a business being profitable but there's a big difference between being profitable and profiteering.

Many corporations have big egos and want to be the biggest, the loudest and the most profitable. This only really impresses a very small minority of people – mainly in the City and on Wall Street – the rest find it either irrelevant or obscene. When Tesco started bragging about how many millions it was making a day what was it really trying to achieve? Did it think that the average Tesco shopper would think, 'wow that's good what a great store'. Maybe what they really thought was, 'Wow, no wonder everything is so expensive these days, this shops making millions out of suckers like me'.

It's easy to get carried away with corporate bragging but in the world of ethics it's not how much you make but HOW you make it. Big profits suggest greed and ruthlessness and send out all the wrong signals. With the recent credit crunch there has been a surge of anti-capitalist articles in national papers. 'Fat Cats' is a term commonly used to describe people who think of nothing but making money. Barclays came under attack from The Sun for attending a conference in Monte Carlo where 'bankers sipped on glasses of champagne that cost £12 while laughing and joking'. No matter what Barclays said the image of greed was fixed in the reader's mind. And no one likes greedy people.

The tendency to think big is best can also be your competitors' advantage. Back in the 1960s (during those Mad Men days) Bill Bernbach's ad agency, DDB, produced a revolutionary strategy for Avis, the car rental company. Hertz was the biggest and most dominant car hire company. It was way ahead of Avis in size, spread and almost everything else. But it had a flaw: corporate arrogance. No one likes arrogance and this alienated people from it. Big and brash is unfriendly. DDB decided to position Avis as a 'challenger brand'. The proposition would capture an ethos – essential to good ethical marketing – and be honest. The line they came up with that said it all was 'When you're number two you try harder'. Pure brilliance. Honest, ethos driven and it says something of value to the customer. Compare that to a common line used by many large corporations 'We're number one'. Who cares? Number one doesn't mean better service or customer satisfaction.

I could name many companies that get it wrong. It's hard for many companies not to boast, it's only human nature. Brands are like people; when they act like the very people we hate the brand loses respect and its reputation is darkened. I always advise clients to think of their brand as a person and to remember that the brand is often a reflection of the people they hire. A bad salesman, clerk or telephone sales person makes a brand look and feel bad. A good one makes them look and feel good. You don't need a degree in psychology to know that.

How many companies value their customers? Not many. Some act like the customer is a nuisance and from personal experience I'd put Ryanair at the top of that list, Talk Talk second and BA third. Top of my good list would be Bosch, Boots and John Lewis. Why? Because they care. They aren't defensive and you can talk to them. They make you feel special and valued; much more so than the money we spend. They act like a friend not a faceless corporation. And what better relationship could you have between a brand and a customer than friendship? Be honest, if your brand was being researched and the consumer described it as a 'best friend' you'd be delighted. If they described it as 'an arrogant git we all hate' you'd be devastated.

Ethics start with an ethos. A desire to do good and to respect people and our environment. Values are an asset and to value just money (and not the customer) is a shallow way of thinking. We all have heard how unhappy rich people can be, as Lennon and McCartney put it, 'money can't buy you love'. I'm not suggesting that an ethical business shouldn't value making money, far from it, it should. Making money means it employs more people, buys more, sells more – all this adds to the economy and society. Successful companies can afford to support communities and help charities. Profit is good. What I am saying is, a company that has tunnel vision has no values, and if it has no values it will do more harm than good.

Ironically, many companies now adopt more environmental practices – recycling, reducing wastage, saving energy, water and paper, thus saving money. There is a financial gain to environmentalism. A representative from Environwise (a company that advises industry on environmental best practice) once told me that they sell their services now on financial gain rather than environmentalism. 'Tell them they can save the planet and they look at you with a blank expression. Tell them they can save money and their eyes light up'. Is that a bad thing? Maybe not if it makes a company greener. The road to conversion starts with small steps not big leaps.

SUMMARY

'Look behind the label' was an M&S campaign but it's also a great philosophy. Sadly, you can't trust everyone to be telling the truth, some NGOs can be just as bad at spin as big brands. Look for the facts and judge for yourself.

Never trust what you read in the newspaper or on many websites. And remember, different people and groups have different ethical values. The public are more interested in what you do than what you say and what you do reflects your ethos. Behaviour defines the brand more than marketing.

4
CHURN AND THE DISPOSABLE SOCIETY

FROM FRIVOLOUS TO FRUGAL – THE END OF CONSUMPTIVE CONSUMERISM

'The era of conspicuous consumption is over', were the words of Andy Boyd, chief executive of ASDA in a recent article in a marketing magazine. Supermarkets, producers and even the world of marketing and advertising are waking up to the fact that the 2008/09 recession could have a fundamental effect upon the future of consumerism, and with it, marketing.

By the end of 2008 business failures like Woolworth's, MFI and Zavvi were hitting the headlines with predictions of 10 major brands going bust in the beginning of 2009.

There's also evidence of new trends being set as ready meal sales slump (by 40% at ASDA) and thermos flask and plastic lunchboxes sales go up. Coffee shops have seen a decline in sales, Starbucks suffering more than most and even sandwich shops are suffering as people start to 'make and take' to work. Even though many people's incomes are not affected – and in fact big discounts are driving down the cost of everything – a more frugal attitude has set in. Many are comparing it to the post-war period.

But with it comes a new sense of community, spirituality and re-evaluation of what matters. Spend, spend, spend is being replaced by a more cautious, thoughtful and questioning attitude.

Those that continue to be frivolous are seen as greedy and immoral. Especially those who drive gas guzzling cars, indulge in expensive tat, consume a lot and waste a lot. A new social attitude is being created: one with higher morals and values.

All of this is bad news for some brands but for the world of ethical marketing it couldn't be better. Churn and fast consumerism is all about indulgence, convenience and 'I buy because I can'. but it's being replaced by considered, conscientious consumerism. A questioning of false promises and spin and a desire for truth and honesty is back in fashion.

For some the recession couldn't be worse. Poor old LG Electronics spent millions on the line 'Life's Good' and then the recession hit and life suddenly wasn't so good. But in a recession life can be good; when you readjust your values you discover new benefits. Suddenly you discover home cooking tastes better, going out less means you spend more time together as a family and eating less indulgent food and walking or cycling instead of driving makes you more fit and healthy.

CHURN AND EARN AND HYPER-CONSUMERISM

'All this buy one get one free, this 3 for 2 stuff really winds me up. It's just a way of inflating prices to encourage excessive consumption. We've come up with a really good alternative which we're very excited about. It's called buy one get one.' Mark Constantine, CEO, Lush Cosmetics

Churn, or Hyper-consumerism, has become the way of the West and is sadly spreading across other countries. The

UK, Europe and America have become consumerholics. We live for shopping; fuelled by the rise of new malls, the internet and by advertising campaigns tempting us to shop till we drop. We are encouraged to own the latest, the fastest, the most exclusive, and occasionally the most eco-ethical. We are encouraged to look and feel like celebrities and thanks to credit we can almost spend like them. Our world is a far cry from the post-war era of just over 60 years ago.

Churn creates demand and no industry has exploited it more than the fashion industry. High Street brands such as Primark and H&M seem to renew stock almost weekly. The production process has increased rapidly and design to shelf is shorter than ever. Many will say this is totally un-necessary, why do we need to change our wardrobe weekly? Of course, the pressure on retailers to produce fast and cheap fashion means that many step over the line – or their suppliers do – unknowingly to the retailer or consumer.

Primark was recently caught with its £5 cotton trousers down when three Indian companies supplying them were discovered to be subcontracting work out to companies that used child labour. Primark denied everything and sacked the three companies. That may have seemed the best reaction but when you're Primark, nothing you can do is right and it drew a great deal of criticism for it meant that hundreds of workers were thrown back into poverty. The best course of action would have been to send monitors in and sort the problem out. Commenting at the time, Martin Hearson, campaign Director of the 'Labour Behind the Label' organisation said: 'cutting and running from suppliers following exposure by campaigners or the media only serves to punish those workers who are brave enough to speak out about their conditions. It certainly won't do any-thing to improve their lives. Such actions make Primark's ethical claims ring hollow'.

It's just another example of the brand's shaky reputation, which the BBC probably summed up best with their programme, 'The Devil Wears Primark'.

WHEN SHOPPING IS BETTER THAN SEX

'Better than sex' was the revelation from one woman in a survey into shopping. Considering that the average woman in her 30s owns 21 handbags and adds a new one every three months (an expenditure of more than £9000 on handbags in a lifetime) and owns on average 30 pairs of shoes, shopping is no cheap thrill. And as our top leisure activity, it now accounts for 37% of all money spent in the UK.

Our addiction to cheap fashionable clothes is a double-edged sword. Churn creates work in developing countries but adds to the exploitation of resources and increases damage to the planet, with fabric being sent to landfill as a consequence and growing concern. But what if we took our fast fashion clothes to recycling centres and passed them on to others in poorer countries. It's a complex argument and what's right and what's wrong can depend upon your viewpoint. There's little doubt that fast churn societies are wealthier, that's why in a recession they want you to spend more.

THE DISPOSABLE SOCIETY

We now live in a world of disposability and in many ways that's the worse churn of all. From plastic cups to paper coffee cups, plastic bags to newspapers, so much of what we handle is binned. It's all very well having recycling bins but the question is why are we throwing so many things away in the first place? If we can have a bag for life what about a cup (see the section on the Battlefront TV programme which I'm involved with) or a Coke bottle for life. As the Shell ad read: 'Away, there is no away'.

For a while making something disposable the first time seemed a good idea. It fitted in with our need for convenience and desire for the instant. Maybe what we need is a new trend in non instant, non convenient products.

The disposable camera seemed a great idea at the time but if you tried to launch it today there'd be a major backlash from environmentalists. Thankfully, technology gave us the film free digital camera and killed it off. Think of all the landfill that has been saved.

MIRROR, MIRROR ON THE WALL ...

But it's not just clothes; vanity products must be one of the ultimate symbols of an affluent over-image conscious society. When Boots, who are a very ethical brand, launched a No. 7 anti-aging cream women queued at the doors. The late Anita Roddick, founder of The Body Shop, would not have approved. Her thoughts are famous: 'The cosmetics industry should be promoting health and wellbeing. Instead, it hypes an outdated notion of glamour and sells false hopes and fantasies'.

MAKE LESS, DESTROY LESS

Over half of all Chinese products are manufactured for foreign companies. Wal-Mart alone imports a tenth of all Chinese goods and is now one of China's largest trading partners. With so much growth in manufacturing (we've all heard the story that they commission a power station every week in China) it has taken over from the US as the biggest producer of CO_2, along with India. All those cheap toys sold in £1 and $1 stores are costing us more than we think. The demise of Woolworth's may have a small benefit after all.

The environment sits heavy as an argument against churn. Make less, destroy less. But that's an environmentalist's argument. Humanitarians will point out how mass production has given millions of people a better life in the developing world. I'm not taking sides here; it's just there are two sides to the people versus planet debate. It's important to differentiate between ethics and politics.

As a brand it's easy to get stuck on one side, or worse, attacked by both sides. Of course the ideal situation would be to mass produce sustainable items that give jobs and wealth to poor people and don't screw up the planet. Many small ethical cloth producers do manage it on a small scale but the numbers employed are fractional compared to those working indirectly for Nike, Primark and even M&S. Take any village in Asia or Africa and I bet they'd rather be making Nike shirts.

Primark, who have become the McDonald's of fashion, and who are portrayed as an evil brand (though they are not alone on the High Street) seem to simply take their punishment and get on with it. Far from sales falling, they seem to be rising, perhaps proving the term 'all publicity is good publicity' to be true. But Primark believes people have a price and if it's cheap enough ethics are left for food shopping (people really do offset that way).

WHITE, BROWN OR GREEN?

Electronics is another industry that has embraced churn. Although it's hard to get people to buy a new washing machine or fridge every year (though lifetime averages are much less) by contrast, the mobile phone industry is rocketing. We now own more than one per head in the UK, with many people having two mobiles.

Every year we throw away more than 5 million mobile phones. The average 18–25 year old changes their mobile phone every nine months, with the average 25 year old changing their handset every 14 months. The life expectancy of an MP3 player is just three years. The electronics industry has managed to make us think in terms of short life spans and uses fashion and upgrades as a marketing device in order to stimulate churn.

The brown and white goods industry has not managed to get us to change our fridges and TVs every six months but we no longer buy anything for life. Recently, I saw an ad for a fridge, 'guaranteed for 10 years'. Just 10 years, my grandfather had his for 30. 'How long is the guarantee', asks the customer, 'one month less than its life expectancy' replied the salesman. But then things are cheaper and that means building things that have lower quality standards. For manufacturers it means they sell more. Churn makes the money go round.

There's a famous Punch cartoon set in the chairman's office of a vacuum cleaner manufacturer. One employee is excited about the fact that a woman has had one of their vacuum cleaners for over 20 years and it's never gone wrong once. 'I don't care how much you offer her but buy it back', exclaims the chairman, 'then I want you to take it apart and find why it's lasted so long and then don't let it happen again'.

The other problem today is that few items are repairable. It's often cheaper to 'sling and buy'. A friend tried to get their oven control panel repaired only to be told the panel would cost more than a new cooker. Apparently men secretly prefer shorter life products as it allows them to upgrade to the latest device. A broken item is an excuse to go to Comet.

Designing products to be green means designing in longevity and there lies a conflict of interest. There have been many improvements in efficiency of manufacture, materials and thanks to energy grading, reduced energy consumption with A, B and C ratings. One argument I heard against longevity was that as equipment gets more efficient year on year those old fridges from a decade ago may still be working but are doing more damage than a new one.

Of course given the EU WEEE (Waste Electrical and Electronic Equipment Regulations) directive manufacturers are now responsible for disposal of products. It's yet to be seen whether they decide to make things last longer in order to reduce costs of recovery or find smarter ways to stop an old washing machine coming back to them, like second life-ing it.

REUSE, REPAIR NOT REPLACE

But now everywhere has become a churn society. Norway is one of the most beautiful places I've been – amazing fjords, glaciers, forest and towns. Regular visits have taught me to see things in contrast. For the last couple of years I've been travelling to Norway to talk on creativity and on ethical marketing. I love the people over there. Their values are well balanced and even though everything is very expensive, they all seem to live full and healthy lives. Their cities are much like any European ones but beyond the city it's a different world, small communities spread across a very large country.

Norway has an ethical dilemma. Before it discovered oil it was relatively poor, now it's wealthy. Its sustainable forests supply a lot of FSC timber. Their homes are far more energy efficient than the average British or American ones.

It was while I was staying on a farm in the Hardanger region that I began discussing with the farmer the differences between Norway and England. We started talking about a broken chair in his living room that despite a missing leg was propped up neatly against a wall. 'In England you'd throw this away and buy another, here we'll repair it'. It's seems a simple statement but in many ways it sums up our life, disposable everything. IKEA has a lot to answer for.

A WINDOW OF OPPORTUNITY – ENCOURAGING CHURN

Many years ago when we worked with Habitat I wrote a new strategy for them entitled 'A window of opportunity'. Habitat had just been taken over by IKEA. The proposal was to encourage people to throw out all that cheesy, cheap, tatty furniture they had (all the stuff that finds its way into our homes and then just lingers there). By encouraging and stimulating churn Habitat could sell more. We even proposed colourful Habitat skips in bright reds, blues, yellows and greens to be placed in key communities. On them would be slogans, 'YOUR CHESTERFIELD TELEPHONE TABLE WOULD LOOK BETTER IN HERE' and 'THE BEST PLACE FOR THAT REAL PLASTIC CUT GLASS BOWL' (we'd actually heard that phrase in Leather Lane market, 'get your real plastic cut glass bowls, just £5'). It seemed like a good idea at the time but now on reflection, it really wasn't ethical. Habitat rejected the proposal but a year later IKEA used an almost identical concept. We'll never know if it was a coincidence or if the proposal was recycled!

Many people believe that in order to improve our environmental status we need to reduce churn. But this is a debate muddied by anti-capitalist arguments. No one doubts that raping the planet to make plastic toys, cheap clothes and mobile phones is justifiable. But manufacturing generates jobs, wealth and better health for millions in the developing world. The real debate questions how can we do it in a sustainable way. 'It doesn't matter how many sandcastles you build if they all get washed back into the sea at night', was a quote I overheard at a conference. Sustainability is the issue, not churn. If we designed fridges to last 30 years there would be fewer people working in the fridge making industry. But what if we designed fridges to have a second life? Richard Featherson of the London Community Recycling Campaign, a most illuminating guy, pointed out to me that the best way to recycle IKEA furniture is to find a new use for it – bedside cabinets can make good rabbit hutches. I really think IKEA should set up a competition for all their designers to design second lives for some of their key products. What a great way to show how ethical you are by taking on the responsibility (a sort of WEEE for furniture) for its next life.

For marketers it's a dilemma. Marketing is after all at the heart of churn, it fuels it but that doesn't make it evil, it's just a tool. Selling to the new consumer is about taking responsibility. If we want to get consumers to change their phone every six months then why not market a collection service that recycles that phone and shows that you care. If you sell fast fashion then set up collection bins for it – if Primark sponsored all those clothes for Africa dump bins think how much better they'd look.

SUMMARY

We have become a society that is dedicated to churn, instant convenience and everything disposable. But society is waking up and starting to reject these ways. There's a return to basics, to old values. As this passes as a wave through communities those brands that haven't adapted will be left out along with all those short-lived items. To the new consumer, brands can be just as disposable as a paper coffee cup.

5
BAD TASTING MEDICINE

FROM BAD TASTING MEDICINE TO GOOD

Gone are the days when we would drink a disgusting tasting medicine because 'it was good for us'. Now we no longer have to suffer; most medicines actually taste good.

The same transition has happened in the ethical market. Where once we had to suffer knobbly vegetables, we now have prettier organic veg. Ugly eco friendly and electric cars have been replaced by stylish ones (well maybe not the Prius yet). Shapeless sack cloth clothes have been usurped by designer brands such as Terra Plana, Work Again, Adili and People Tree (who are fast gaining a reputation for their fashion as well as their ethics). Or urban wear brands like Howies, THTC, Kuyichi and one of the most innovative brands, Junky Styling.

Fairtrade has had to shrug off an image of poor taste because in the beginning its product was perceived as poor quality. Sitting next to two (more mature) ladies on the train to Edinburgh – where I was doing a talk on ethical market-ing – I chatted to them about their shopping basket; what they bought, what they thought and how they felt about ethical products and brands. A small sample, but never underestimate the importance of speaking to real people rather than relying on research groups. When it came to Fairtrade I was shocked by their response. 'Oh that's that horrible tea and coffee they give after church on Sundays'. They liked what it stood for but felt there was too much of a compromise on quality. And I have to agree. When I started working with Traidcraft back in 2002 all of us in the office were less than impressed with the taste of the coffee (though the biscuits were great). To be fair, things have improved dramatically and Café Direct now wins awards for its taste and their tea is just as good as any.

THE PRICE OF BEING ETHICAL

However, prices still remain high and many retailers have positioned ethical products as premium. Because they see ethical values as added value, they believe it can command a higher price. The average retail mark up is 2.5 × the buyer's price. As many ethical products cost more to buy in the first place the difference, once multiplied by 2.5, makes it expensive, which in turn, reduces the chances of it selling. Simple economics of supply and demand will tell you that as price goes up demand goes down, which is not good for fair trade. If an ordinary t-shirt costs £7 and an ethical one cost £10 you'd see them on the rack for £17.50 and £25. More sensibly, why not just add the difference, being £3 and sell at £20.50? Same profit, but the likelihood of selling more is increased. Simple economics really.

FAIRTRADE – A FAIR PRICE?

One area that's seen a price equalization is Fairtrade tea and coffee. It's now possible to buy Fairtrade certified tea at the same price as traditional brands. When FFI (Fine Foods International), one of the biggest suppliers of instant Fairtrade coffee, launched Fair Instant they positioned it at the same price level as Nescafé. Which makes for an easy choice – ethical or unethical? They also donated 20p to Save the Children per jar. It's not surprising that product sales rate soon overtook others in the category.

However, with a recession one of the first areas to suffer is premium. This is an effect most notable in the organic industry. The late 2008 credit crunch has created a change in attitude, resulting in people spending less. One researcher told me about a shopper who was no longer buying the organic brand (fronted by a well known chef) and had started buying the own label as it was cheaper. Yet her income was no less, she didn't really need to save money (as good as that was) but felt the need to change her ways. 2009 will see indulgent premium brands suffer and some will go to the wall. However, the other effect is that super-markets are looking for space to put cheaper sourced products on the shelves. Products that are premium or marginal sellers get elbowed off, often the more ethical ones, replaced by those with a dubious origin.

A RETURN TO POST-WAR VALUES

The recession may well be driving us back to post-war values, but it opens up new opportunities. Recycling and reusing are becoming fast emerging trends. Brands like Junky Styling, Worn Again and Terra Plana were born out of the idea of 'make use not make waste'. There's a growing movement in Australia that encourages people to turn any-thing back into clothes, from curtains to carpets.

Junky Styling was started in 1997 by Kerry Seager and Annika Sanders after spotting the trend in recycled materials and the desire for individuality. They deconstruct second-hand clothes and re-work them into new, unique garments, with no two being alike. They now even offer a bespoke service to those who want to give their old clothes a second life.

Terra Plana and Worn Again produce a great range of boots and shoes using fabrics as diverse as prison blankets, bicycle tyres, parachutes, seat belts and seat covers from Virgin planes. Remarkable produce stationery products from tyres, plastic cups and CDs with the source as part of the design, like 'I used to be a plastic box'. There's also been a big growth in corporate gifts made from old materials. When society and business put their minds to it suddenly 'one man's rubbish is another man's gold' takes on a real meaning. There is money in recycling and new businesses are being set up all the time.

SECOND LIFE PACKAGING

Maybe it's something to do with growing up as part of the Blue Peter generation but when I look at an empty washing up liquid bottle I see a space rocket, a cornflake packet as a house and an empty bean can as one half of a communication device.

As an adult I rediscovered my imagination for recycling when I had kids; a kitchen roll tube became too good to throw away. We had a cupboard dedicated to old packets, plastic containers and metal lids. Sooner or later they would become anything from a telescope to a space station. Thanks to this cupboard (and a little help from me) my son won the fancy dress competition with his robot suit.

There's little doubt that food and other household products are over packaged. In some cases there's little room for change – health and safety regulations, security and economics dictate a lot of packaging. But why does anyone need to have their bottles of water wrapped again in plastic and then put in a plastic carrier bag? This was just one example that was entered into The Independent's hall of shame, part of their campaign against over packaging.

For many people the answer is to just stick it in the recycle bin. But maybe if we applied a little imagination we could do more interesting things with our surplus containers. At the risk of sounding like a train spotter, egg cartons make great seed growers. Just add a little soil, plant a seed and when it's started to grow plant the container straight into the ground (the roots will grow through the base). One shoe company has taken this idea further and packaged its shoes in a box made of the same material as egg cartons and have included a pack of seeds.

If manufacturers aren't willing to reduce their packaging they could be encouraged to see packaging as having a second life. Glass bottles are often plain ugly, yet if they were designed to look like a vase, more would end up around the home. When you consider that up to 25% of your shopping is packaging, it's such a simple way to convey to the consumer your ethical values. Gü may not be fair trade or organic but by leaving you with a useful glass jar, rather than a plastic pot, you feel it's more worthy.

I am amazed that when packaging is considered such an essential element of marketing no one has jumped on the idea of using second life packaging as brand value. In a marketplace of so many 'me too' brands it would act as a differentiator. With one cleaning product range we were advising on we recommended that for their home delivery range they put the products in a box that could be reused for kids' play. Each box would be printed to look like a different building so kids could collect a whole range. This also emphasized how naturally safe the cleaning products were, and encouraged repeat purchase.

It was The Body Shop who, out of necessity rather than an eco mission, encouraged their customers to bring back the bottle. Of course this wasn't new, for generations fizzy drinks have been sold in glass bottles that carried a deposit which you'd get back when you returned the bottle. Why do we not adopt this method again? What we need is a national recycle, return financial incentive. A sort of packaging tax; you pay when you buy and get a refund when you return.

Various methods have been explored but one supermarket that linked it to points claimed it was poorly supported. Or maybe it was just poorly marketed? Budgens (Crouch End), a leading thinker in ethics among supermarkets, adopts the 'bring a shopping bag back get pennies off your shopping' approach. It works for them. They also provide a packaging recycling bin for customers.

Of course, some eco brands have adopted the refill method, from water to detergents but it's messy and not very practical in big stores where spills can cause a major accident.

Over packaging and failure to design in reuse are major problems facing manufacturers, and not just those in the FMCG (fast moving consumer goods) area but also white and brown goods and office equipment. Bizarrely and ironically, I remember receiving a huge box from a stationery supplier, packed full of bubble wrap, all for just five A5 'Remarkable' recycled note books. Now that's over packaging.

SUMMARY

Many businesses have discovered that being more ethical saves them money; that reducing waste reduces costs. And some have discovered that their waste has value. Others, like Remarkable, have made a business from turning waste into new exciting objects. Hand in hand with this is the need to treat people fairly and with respect. It all makes for a better business. But be prepared to challenge conventional thinking, to embrace change and invest in new values. It may even redefine your business and open up new areas for growth. If you're not changing with the times you'll be left behind and vanish.

6
IT'S NOT WHAT YOU SAY BUT WHAT YOU DO

DOING THE WALK AND TALK OF ETHICS

Marketing and especially advertising and PR rely on the 'what' you say. Agencies may defend themselves by stating the fact that they have no control over the product (or service) but challenge a client who is paying them to do the talk without the walk. What is more influential than most advertising in creating a brand's reputation is what it does. You can't behave one way and say something different. It's important in the world of ethical marketing to make sure that the *way* and *say* are aligned.

Consumers won't be talking positively about those funny million dollar TV ads for your bank if you upset them with an aggressive letter or if staff in the local branch are rude or lazy. Wasting the customer's time is another factor that angers many customers and too many companies do it. Ethics isn't just about the planet and fair trade but about showing respect for people, your customer being one of them. Their time is just as valuable as yours.

If there are two key words that seem to come through they are honesty and respect. I recommend that you write them on the office wall and ask 'does my business tick these two boxes? Does the way we deal with suppliers, staff and customers tick these two boxes? Does our marketing reflect these two words?'

Many companies may not think they have an ethical message but honesty can be a very powerful way to engage people, even if you aren't saving the rainforest. You don't need to be holier than thou, after all given the eco-ethical political views of some people, it's impossible to be perfect. Honesty is a very ethical value and fundamental to trust. And trust is the most important word in marketing – blow that and you've blown your brand, your reputation and your customer relations.

GOOD OLD HONEST FOOD

I'm always one for a bit of controversy, especially because it challenges people's thinking and ideas, which is exactly what I want to do. Is ethics all about the environment and charity or is it about truth? Can a product that doesn't have any obvious benefit to mankind other than as fuel be ethical? If oil companies were really honest could we cope with that?

Imagine a typical episode of The Simpsons. Homer is having a dilemma. He's woken up to climate change and is feeling guilty about driving his car and all the products we use that come from oil. He turns on the TV and there's a man from an oil company being interviewed. The green activist is having a go: 'Be honest Mr Richy, your oil company is raping the planet; you are getting rich off the resources of the earth'.

Mr Richy bows his head: 'You're right. I should be honest'. The interviewer and green activist looks shocked. Homer looks puzzled: 'Look guys it's true, we suck oil out of the ground so you can drive your cars, get your groceries delivered to your home, take the kids in buses to schools and fly on holiday. It provides electricity, is used to make plastic and everything important. If we stopped tomorrow your life would be in ruins. The world economy would collapse and the world would fall into poverty. Scotland, Norway, the Middle East would step back 500 years. People would die, suffer and we'd have wars. Sure we make $100m a day but you pay us that. We are just meeting your demand. Sure it's going to run out but we're not stupid. We have millions of people to pay every week. That's why we're investing billions into the next fuel technology; we have a business to run. Go on condemn me. I'm a bad guy'. I can see the dropped jaws bouncing off the coffee tables of the public. I can see Homer being emotionally moved and saying: 'Gee, the man's right. Actually he's not so bad after all'.

Spam is a great product. This could be my Ratner moment! Great in the sense that it's survived for decades and even despite the move by consumers to more natural and ethical foods, it's still selling well and growing in some markets. Surprisingly, it's very popular in Japan. It was also very popular with a dog named Lucky we worked with for the More Than Insurance group (there's a market no one's considered). And it actually tastes nice (I think).

Now I can hear the cries from vegetarians that Spam isn't ethical, it's processed pork with water and sugar in it. But the one thing Spam is, is honest. It doesn't try to pretend to be green, organic or use spin terms like 'corn fed pigs'. You know what it is and what you are getting. And unless you are selling to a hippie commune, the general public like to mix up their shopping basket with the good, the bad and the ugly. The worse thing they can put in is something they think is holy but which is really the food equivalent of the devil.

It's well known by those that have worked with me that I have always wanted to win the Spam account and market it to youth – those people that eat lots of kebabs and pizzas late at night. It's a lot healthier than a kebab and has fewer calories than a pizza. It's full of protein so is actually good for you (but like anything, in moderation). Cooked up with two eggs it makes for a good breakfast and has less fat than cheap bacon or sausages. And of course, it's given its name to one of the best theatre shows in London, Spamalot. Unfortunately it's also been used to describe unwanted emails – I never did get the connection.

I've used Spam for D&AD student workshops as it's a great product for a reframing exercise. Take it from a food for poor old ladies to a fun, funky product for youth (worked for Pot Noodles). I even created a speculative campaign with attitude (important in youth marketing), ALL MEAT. NO VEG. One script features Dave arriving at his mate's house with his girlfriend Mandy: 'I forgot to tell you, Mandy's vegetarian'. His mate pauses for a moment: 'No problem'. He lets Dave in and shuts the door in Mandy's face leaving her outside: 'Spam. All meat. No veg'. Cut to Dave tossing a bit of cheese out of the window.

THINK GREAT, BE HONEST, FEEL PROUD

Now some people may be shocked that an ethical marketing expert would sell Spam (and mock vegetarians) but its British humour and its marketing. No one is lying. No one is trying to pull a green pullover over the product. In marketing we have to face reality. There are good things like Fairtrade coffee and tea. There are bad things like oil and weapons. And there are most things in between. As a nation we are not all pure and good and yes, we abuse our bodies – just look at cigarettes, fatty foods and alcohol.

My message here is not about the environmental or people debate but about honesty. The one thing I keep saying is tell it as it is, don't lie. I have a slogan on my office wall THINK GREAT, BE HONEST, FEEL PROUD. Recently, I've added KEEP IT SIMPLE.

If you can get a copy, watch 'Crazy People' with Dudley Moore. He's an ad executive who has a break down and ends up in a mental institute. He starts to get the residents to do ads and creates a new form of advertising that shocks Madison Avenue – honest advertising. Volvo: 'It's boxy and boring but reliable'; Qantas: 'We've never crashed a plane yet'. One day I intend to scamp all the ads up and put them on a website.

Before I finally move away from Spam I'd recommend that everyone visit the US site www.spam.com – it's brilliant. It's fun, totally mad in places and very kitsch. You can even buy a wide range of merchandise – Spam boxer shorts, ties, fancy dress outfits, bags, the list is endless. In the US it is well marketed and they've managed to sell it as a BBQ food. In the UK it still sells to the over 50s who buy four cans a year, yawn, though it's recently found a new popularity as a pizza topping (probably eaten by students). I bet if you put a can in every kitchen in all the halls of residence in colleges and supported it with an engaging campaign that was in tune with students' mentality (like ALL MEAT. NO VEG) it would fly off the shelves. Mark my words, gut instinct is rarely wrong.

ABBEY NATIONAL AND HABITAT

There is no greater shame in branding than when your brand is re-christened by the public to reflect how they feel about you. Abbey Shabby and Shabby Tat are two examples.

The public aren't stupid. The public aren't stupid. I've repeated that because the evidence suggests that many brands think they are. It's simple, if you try and con people into thinking you have a good service and you don't, they find out. Branding isn't, contrary to what some branding agencies say, about the image you wish to project but about how people see you. While a well-known telephone company attempts to portray itself as a customer friendly brand, the reality is very different. Its salesmen lie, its service is terrible and its customer support is one of the worst of any telecoms company. Search for their name on the web and numerous blogs and sites attacking them pop up. They obviously ignore it all as when I wrote a blog on a marketing site they didn't even pick it up (something any decent PR company would have done). Talk is cheap (well actually most brands spend millions on it) but actions deliver an experience and experience is far more influential in shaping opinion than a nice logo and a funny TV campaign.

I employ three views of branding when I'm working on a brand project:

OUTWARD BRANDING – this is the image you are trying to portray. Expressed through graphics, advertising and marketing materials, retail design, even your vans.

REFLECTIVE BRANDING – this is what people say they think and feel once they see it. So often brands fail to research and evaluate this properly. Your nice graphics may look good but what does the consumer really think? Actually, forget think, it's what they feel that matters because that's an emotional take out. If you have a problem your nice new graphics may not be the solution you were hoping for. It may even add to it.

BRAND REPUTATION – this is not what you say but what consumers say about you. No amount of fancy graphics can fix a brand the public are feeling bad about. In the City shareholders use the word 'reputation'. Marketers use the term 'brand'. I recommend the term 'brand reputation'.

Abbey tried to rebrand themselves out of a hole. They spent millions on a new identity, logos signage and retail as well as clever, expensive ads and nice new literature. The new multi-coloured logo has a lower case (which was a trend at the time). It was meant to look modern and fresh. But modern and fresh wasn't what people wanted. Abbey missed the one thing that got them a bad reputation – shabby customer service. From my own experience, I found the service less than good.

It was said that Richard Branson made a very powerful statement when he was doing battle with British Airways: 'While BA spends millions telling people how great they are I spend my millions making Virgin a great airline. I'll let the people tell others if they think we're great or not'. Those are the words of a very smart person who really understands people and therefore marketing. Having worked with BA my own impression at the time was of a company who thought if they threw money around and said how great they were enough times, it would stick. It didn't. Time and again it came out as anything but the world's favourite airline (this term was a spin on how many people flew and was actually dishonest).

During this period I was to be sent to Chicago on BA, on to New York on American Airlines and to return on Virgin in order to make a comparison. This was all part of a brief for BA business class. At check-in I was bounced from business class to standard. It took a lot of explaining to get the check-in staff to understand that I needed to travel business class because I was working on a marketing campaign for business class. Finally, I got my seat back. No apology. First impression – the staff are unfriendly, unhelpful and rude.

On the plane it was just as bad. Could I get the attention of the hostess – my mouth was dry and I really needed water. Finally I had to go into the galley and help myself. Suddenly a school teacher voice behind me cried, 'sir you're not allowed in here'. I explained my problem but the far from sympathetic response I got was 'you'll just have to wait like everyone else'. Second impression – not good.

The American Airlines flight was a flying bus with little to comment on. The staff were friendly but it was a short trip. However, in New York BA had failed to confirm the room. It was eleven at night, the hotel was full and there was no 24 hour helpline I could call to sort it out. I ended up walking the streets looking for another hotel. Next day I did get an apology and lots of excuses that it was all the hotel's fault.

By stark contrast Virgin couldn't do enough. We had a delayed start and even though it was no fault of Virgin's they apologized to all the passengers. The staff were amazingly friendly and service was faultless. There was even a masseur on board. At Heathrow I was informed my car was waiting: 'Car?' 'Yes sir, it will take you to wherever you want to go'. All part of the service. 'Wow!' That's what you get when you put the marketing budget into the service.

On my return to the office I had a problem; how to sell a bad service when your competitor has an excellent one. Thankfully I didn't have to worry. The brief had been cancelled while I was away. I have to admit this was during a period when BA was tripping over its own toes; it's a lot better now. Well so I'm told and I believe my friends over any ad.

Research has shown that people trust people. Even people we don't know. We actually don't trust ads. Why would we? We all know they are trying to sell us something. No one truly trusts a salesman. That's a bit of a dilemma if you are trying to advertise an honest message. How can you tell the truth if no one trusts the channel? The simple answer is use another channel.

KEEP IT SIMPLE AND HONEST

One highly ethical client I really enjoyed working with was the FPA (Family Planning Association). We've done some great work, and won many awards, all thanks to two factors: the client was brave and understood their audience.

Sexual health is a sensitive area. It's easy to do cheap 18–30 style gags but much harder to achieve responsible powerful communication. There's a fine line between fun and trivializing things. It's also easy to preach and that really fails. Trying to connect with the audience is not easy so you need to understand how they think and feel.

In 2002, after leaving Saatchi & Saatchi, I set up a new creative agency. Based on Mad Dogs and Englishmen meets Mother we set out to do work that wasn't formulaic, but creative and different. We followed Mother in not having traditional suits but invested in talent in the form of creatives. But a new agency needs to launch with impact. Our first two campaigns were for FPA and Traidcraft.

FPA didn't have much money and a traditional ad campaign (or even a viral) was out of the question. Sometimes too much money reduces creativity, when you have less of a budget you need to think smarter.

We decided to go for a stunt and have a little fun in the process; so we put a 21 foot condom on the Cerne Abbis Giant (the large chalk figure of a man with a large erect penis carved on a hill side in Dorset).

Having an idea is one thing, selling it is another, especially when you are going to mess with a national monument. We pointed out to the client that we could get arrested. 'We have lawyers' was the reply. Can you imagine a bank saying that?

We managed to pull off the stunt on a very small budget, with the help of a mate who trains the SAS and lots of plastic from Homebase. And thankfully without getting arrested or any angry letters from the National Trust who manage the monument. FPA got lots of publicity on a global scale (we even got a mention in The Sun). Pictures appeared as far away as America, India and Australia, and even in a Thai newspaper.

Colleges are interesting places. Full of over sexed individuals all in their prime. Nature couldn't get a better breeding ground. Add to that alcohol and drugs and intent soon becomes the regret of the morning after. STIs (sexually transmitted infections) are spreading fast. Unwanted pregnancies are another problem. It's a tough brief to convince people to use condoms, let alone even carry them.

SELLING SEX ADVICE THROUGH THE TURN OF A COIN

Among students, ads are seen as authoritative – your dad, the state, teacher. These kids have just escaped their authority figures, the last thing they respond to is preaching. In many colleges you'll see lectures on A3 posters, some from our nanny state. Ironically, they can do more to encourage the opposite behaviour and push kids to rebel.

For a new sexual health campaign to encourage students to use condoms we needed to find a new channel (like before, we had very little budget) and so decided to use ambient media. What better than a coin placed on the floor of canteens and bars; every student would pick it up.

The client suggested £1 coins, we thought 10p was enough. So we placed thousands of 10p coins on the floors of over 95 colleges across the UK.

When picked up on the back was a sticker with the line, SOME THINGS YOU CAN'T HELP PICKING UP. HIV OR A STI SHOULDN'T BE ONE OF THEM. The campaign was backed up by small posters near public telephones in the colleges and on notice boards, highlighting the confidential help line. We also ran beer mats and placed small cards in empty cigarette packs – we'd noticed that smokers can't help but to shake an empty pack left on a bar in the hope there's a cigarette in it. The card gave that impression.

Reaction to the campaign was great. It got better recall than the government one at the time and another by the Terrence Higgins Trust. Feedback told us that it felt honest and wasn't trying to preach. It was clever, engaging – people showed it to others and it started discussions – and was very different (no one had used a coin as an ad before, many have since).

To deliver effective health messages you have to understand the psychology of responsibility. Don't take it away from people, don't demand or tell them and never chastise them. Educate and advise, empower and respect them, and they'll respond. But most of all; be honest. Twisting statistics to scare people backfires because then no one believes them. Telling people there's 5000 dangerous chemicals in a cigarette is unbelievable. Focusing on just three is scary. Saying smoking can make your limbs falls off is laughable because no one knows anyone who has lost a limb. Keep it real. Statistics may be persuasive in a college for accountants but the rest of the student population aren't swayed by them.

Interestingly, no coins turned up in the machines or bars of one college we tested.

NAPPY FAMILIES – GETTING YOUR MESSAGE TO STUDENTS

We followed the coin campaign a year later with an 'avoid an unwanted pregnancy' campaign. In one college we worked with (London College of Communication (LCC – formerly LCP)) we got the marketing course students to do surveys and post campaign evaluations.

The shocking outcome was just how many girls get pregnant in the first term. This may be understandable – freedom, alcohol, lots of good looking fit guys and parties.

The students helped us identify the triggers. In response we mailed hundreds of nappies to students in halls. On the nappy was a simple message, IT'S A LOT EASIER TO PUT ON A CONDOM. Simple, honest and to the point. It also scored highly with students in post campaign research.

The campaign consisted of 3D posters (with real nappies on), direct mail, events and an email campaign. The students really got into the campaign and even dressed up in large nappies to distribute leaflets (novel if not a bit unusual, but that's campus life for you). We did investigate using the fire alarm system – it has a speaker system rather than a bell – we wanted to broadcast a crying baby at 6 in the morning, but the college Health & Safety officials stamped on that one.

After the campaign we conducted a post campaign survey, awareness was very high and comments on the campaign were all positive. We asked what had happened to all the real nappies. Seems a lot of boys put them on their teddy bears!

THE POWER OF YOUTH MEDIA – THE POSTCARD

Forget the glamorous world of TV ads or big posters, try postcards. I challenge most people to do a good one; posters are easy by comparison, as they are big and in your face. Postcards are small and have to work very hard to get noticed and picked up. But once they are, they stay with people, something posters don't. I was speaking at a charity convention and showed a novel campaign we did for FPA, 'FPA by another name'. One of the audience members told me afterwards that she still had the postcards pinned up above her desk after two years. That's advertising with longevity.

A good place to talk to people about sexual health is in bars and clubs. I'm a great fan of those free postcards run by Boomerang. They are very effective and cheap. Best of all they challenge you to do advertising in a different way. Advertising works on the disruptive principle. It disrupts your magazine, your TV programmes, your vision. It's like that annoying waiter who interrupts you in a restaurant when you are romantically engaged with your partner. Disruption is an outdated idea and one reason people dislike ads. I use a simple thought in my seminars and workshops; if you had to put a price tag on your advertising and sell it, how many people would buy it. The answer is almost always no one. So let's apply honesty to our industry for a controversial moment.

People don't really like ads; only the few really silly, funny or clever ones. When 24 transferred to commercial TV, apparently, many people stopped watching it because the ads ruined the programmes' roller coaster ride. Watch most people reading a magazine and they skip the ads. Why? Because they're dull, too rational and non-engaging. In the States, part of the success of the 'X-Files'-like TV series 'Fringe' (brilliant series) was to reduce the number of ads during the programme and sell less for more. Everyone's a winner, the viewer, the advertiser and Fox's media salesmen.

Postcards in bars are a form of permission marketing. No one has to pick them up. No one thrusts them into your hand, if they're good enough they'll get taken. And that's measurable. In fact, when agencies just stick ads on them they tend to fail. One Boomerang sales rep told me he was advising the agency of a well known car brand that he didn't think their postcards would work: 'They are just the poster on a postcard'. The arrogant account handler from the agency replied: 'yes but they've won a D&AD'. They ignored the rep's advice and didn't manage to win over the consumers. Few were picked up.

One of the other things postcards in bars do is satisfy the three most important rules of media: RIGHT PLACE; RIGHT TIME; RIGHT FRAME OF MIND. In sexual health you have key windows of opportunity to connect with people. There's no point talking to people about condoms over breakfast, better to discuss the morning after pill. It's during the evening in bars and clubs that the sexual journey starts.

We produced a fun postcard with a naked man on it. Where his manhood was we cut out a finger size hole. On the back, a simple line. DON'T FORGET ITS NATIONAL CONDOM WEEK. No lecture. No nanny state trying to shame you into using condoms or patronizingly suggesting that you want respect. People picked up the cards and played with them. Finger out, and everyone has a laugh. Now here's the bit that may surprise some people. Humour sells more than just beer. It's actually one of the best ways to talk to people about sensitive issues, especially sex. The cards started a conversation and made people think for themselves and that's what good marketing should do. Empower the consumer, don't disempower them.

Sexual health is a great ethical cause and it gives you great satisfaction, knowing you may have prevented an unwanted baby, or saved someone from a sexually transmitted disease.

SUMMARY

Keep it simple. Keep it honest. Talk to people at the right time, in the right place and when they are in the right frame of mind.

Get out of the ivory tower of marketing and back to the floor. Talk to real people, not via research groups, and you'll discover the truth about how people think and feel. Remember that they both think (logical) and feel (emotional). And if they think badly of your brand they'll feel the same way, and vice versa. And finally, if you are going to do high visibility advertising, don't pollute the mass media with rubbish. I commented on the Post Office ads in one Post Office and the counter staff told me the staff hated the campaign. If your staff hates the ads, so will the public. I recently read that the public loves just 5% of ads, hates 7% and ignores the rest. So be the best.

7
BRAND TERRORISM

DAVID AND GOLIATH

'A kid with a six hundred dollar laptop can bring down a six million dollar campaign'. I've put this quote in many blogs to highlight a factor I call 'Brand Terrorism'. These may seem like strong words but you can't underestimate the power of social networking, especially when the truth goes against the marketing message. The truth, whether it's used maliciously or just factually, can hurt.

Just take the case of Kryptonite bike locks. They made great locks that couldn't be broken. Well, that was what they thought until someone posted an online video of one of their U-locks being opened with a simple Bic pen. Disaster. Word spread and the company fell into a big black hole.

'Look behind the label' was M&S's early campaign, but if we really looked behind many brands we wouldn't like what we saw – even the ethical ones, sorry the ones we think are ethical (there is a difference). It's impossible to tick all the boxes. Big corporate brands can only do so much and it's almost impossible to be ethically pure, especially if your main focus is delivering more profit year on year to your shareholders. Even People Tree have to fly clothes in, innocent and The Body Shop have to use packaging and transport their bottles by trucks.

HOW TO AVOID ANTI-BRAND WASH

If you're looking for some eco dirt it's easy to find one small point (an ethical Achilles heel) and use it to have a go. The Sun attacked Starbucks with the front cover headline 'Starberks' (6 October 2008) and another inside, 'The great drain robbery'.

You may well be expecting a shock horror story about abuse of workers in the Third World or demolishing rainforests, but no. The issue was over a small low pressure water tap that sits behind the counter and is used to clean spoons. It's left running continuously and as a consequence (according to figures from the Sun) an estimated 23.4 million litres of water goes down the drain every day – enough to fill an Olympic swimming pool every 83 minutes and which would provide enough water to supply the drought ridden population of Namibia.

Most people will be thinking 'Namibia, where's that?' (it's the place next to South Africa where Angelina Jolie and Brad Pitt went so Angelina could have her baby). Namibia generally attracts eco-tourists with the majority visiting to experience the different climates and natural geographical landscapes such as the great eastern desert and plains. There's lots of desert there. The population is just 1 987 000 (2003 census). 'Millions of gallons down plughole, enough to keep a country alive', reads the sub-headline but now you've looked behind the Sun's label you can see how they are using it to spin their version of the story. We've all heard of 'greenwash'; here's 'anti-brandwash'.

Smarter people will be thinking, 'yes, but that water can't be transported to Namibia, it's an irrelevant comparison'. However, the Sun does point out that in drought ridden Australia, taps are also running – oops! Starbuck's handled the story very badly and didn't manage their shops well. On the day I visited a Starbucks in central London and asked to see the famous tap, the woman looked puzzled. Finally it clicked: 'oh no, not another one' she replied. By contrast, when Pret were attacked for selling a share to McDonald's they briefed all their staff on how to respond to customers, which was very smart.

FROM HUMANITARISM TO PLANETARISM

Consumers are not stupid, they are becoming better informed and able to make their own judgements. We need to remember that one person's ethics are not another's. As highlighted in other sections, there are two distinct areas people fall into, humanitarism and planetarism, and there are many issues within those two simple areas, just take animal welfare for example.

The power of the web for good and bad is just amazing. What starts as a small group can soon become massive and so influential big brands have to listen. One example is ColaLife, created by Simon Berry. It all started as an idea on Facebook and exploded. Berry has been trying to get Coke to use their vast distribution network to help deliver life-saving medications and information in developing countries. This concept, ColaLife, could help save hundreds of thousands of people (www.colalife.org).

Amusingly, one of Coke's great straplines, when translated into one of the Chinese languages, reads 'bring your dead back to life'. Now, more seriously, brands like Coke, Pepsi (and many other mass distributed products) could soon be the new saviours, preventing millions of deaths from water related illnesses. According to WaterAid, one billion people lack access to clean water and every day 5000 children die as a result of drinking dirty water. In many regions of the world people have to walk miles to get water. Water that's often dirty, polluted or infected with disease, as it's often shared with animals.

Quoting Simon Berry: 'Our idea is that Coca-Cola could use their distribution channels (which are amazing in developing countries) to distribute rehydration salts to the people that need them desperately. Maybe by dedicating one compartment in every 10 crates as "the life saving compartment"?' Gives new meaning to Coke's famous straplines, 'Life tastes good' and 'Coke adds life'.

WaterAid is not a great fan of distributing rehydration salts for treating diarrhoea (it's a short-term solution) preferring to educate people about hygiene and putting in proper sanitation and clean water supplies. But Simon's campaign is gathering a mass of supporters by using the power of Web 2.0 and social networking to spread the word and create a digital community of activists (almost 4000 have joined the open group on Facebook).

This case illustrates how one person can very quickly gain enough momentum to be as powerful as a major charity in applying pressure to large corporations. This is a new concept of David and Goliath. Whereas the old model placed charities as the champions of a particular issue or cause, now any passionate, driven member of the public can soon gather a force behind them and push for change. There is some evidence that issue sites are gaining more followers than traditional charity sites in the States. Could common causes replace charitable organizations as the main influencers in the future?

AVOIDING BRAND SUICIDE

When the newspapers discovered that one brand was paying as little as 7 p an hour to workers in sweat shops and that Primark were using sweatshops in Manchester (revealed by an undercover BBC reporter) it made national headlines. Forget all the expensive glossy adverts and banners in-store claiming ethical values, the reputation of a brand is defined in the consumers' minds by those headlines.

After years of the media digging up the dirt and NGOs spying on these factories, you have to ask, just how dumb are the big brands like Primark, Tesco and ASDA? They all run very good businesses; no one can fault them for that (in 2007 Primark made a £233m profit). However, given the appetite for a negative human interest story – the press, charities and NGOs are all looking for those who are playing dirty and exploiting people – you'd think that their CSR department would have more influence and power. One bad headline can undo a million pound ad campaign in minutes. Worse, as journalists rarely get it factually correct, you are probably open to worse damnation than what you deserve.

Primark, ASDA and Tesco were all named in the press as exploiting people in Bangladesh by War on Want, who for an extra PR angle, decided to encourage workers to take legal action against those retailers in the UK.

When the BBC sent an undercover reporter into factories in Manchester that were paying less than the minimum wage and making people work long hours in bad conditions it made both the national TV news and the press. The phrase 'what's the real cost of cheap fashion?' has been used many times in articles and has become a term parents are using now to comment on their kids buying from Primark and other discount stores. Neil Kearney from the International Textile Worker's Federation (which looks after workers) made a power slogan comment in the press 'There's no such thing as cheap clothing'.

'I do not think the customers of Primark want to get their clothes at the expense of other people's lives', was a comment made by Manchester City Centre Chief Councillor Pat Karney (TNS Knitwear was the factory in Manchester investigated by the BBC).

Phrases like these stick and enter the language of the consumer. They are powerful and act like negative slogans, sometimes for generations. As if it wasn't bad enough, Primark had been discovered to be using sweatshops – a year before the BBC had linked them to factories using child labour – and they were forced to take down any in-store claims about their so called ethical policy by the Ethical Trading Initiative (who don't want to list their members on their website).

These are prime (or maybe Primark) examples of 'brand suicide'. While one side of the business is trying to do good another isn't. It demonstrates why having a joined up ethos is important. Branding is far more than a nice corporate identity, it's all about brand ethos – the WHY behind the WHAT and HOW you do things. If everyone knows the WHY then the rest follows. But if the WHY is just 'buy it cheap, make money' you get abuse.

A BITTER AFTER TASTE

War on Want, Action Aid, Greenpeace, Friends of the Earth, WWF, The Guardian and the BBC are all brands we trust, so when they condemn a big corporate brand it's even worse, especially as everyone reports it. The damage to brand reputation is immense and sometimes takes years to undo. Nestlé and Barclays still suffer decades after incidents of bad behaviour, Nestlé over its milk scandal and debt collection and Barclays for South Africa.

There's a saying in marketing: 'the sweet taste of low prices is soon replaced by the bitter taste of poor quality'. A more updated version would be: 'the sweet taste of low prices is soon replaced by the bitter taste of a brand reputation destroyed'.

There's no smoke without fire and all of these brands are defending themselves; however the damage is done and you can't help thinking that Primark's prices are hardly possible without exploitation. No doubt heads will roll and procurement and CSR advisors may well be getting their P45s. The public may love a discount but the growing awareness of ethics means that the consumer is shopping with a conscience.

Even given a recession, surveys reveal that we are actually becoming more people and community focused not less. Environmentalism may be old news for the media but people aren't.

WHO PAYS? THE POWER OF THE PEOPLE

In a BBC programme looking at cotton it was revealed that a retailer buys a t-shirt for less than $1.50 and sells it for $5. The rest is profit (the average mark up is 2.5 × cost). When you look at the chain, it's shocking how little the farmer and farm worker get. Even more shocking when you consider there are many millions of poor people earning less than a dollar a day.

Action Aid's brilliant WHO PAYS? campaign has been one of the most successful in recent years to challenge supermarkets about exploiting Third World labour. It asked a simple question, 'who's paying for the discount?' and 'when you pick up an apple do you think about who picked it off the tree?' With over 42 000 people signing up to their loyalty card, Action Aid proved that the public does care and can make a difference. The campaign forced Sainsbury's to announce in their ads that they were paying for discounts on bananas.

Supermarkets are quick to claim that they listen to their shoppers' desires but do they really? Is selling unethically sourced products responding to the customers' desire for cheap food or the supermarkets' desire for more profit?

THE ETHICAL TIME BOMB

Another example of brand suicide is the behaviour of banks in the recession and the failure of some banks to pass on rate decreases. The UK's biggest lender, HBOS, would only pass on 0.25 of a percentage point after one reduction by the Bank of England. When the recession ends those financial institutes that put their 'greed before the public need' will all be paying a bigger price – mark my words, it's an ethical time bomb.

The public and press will not forgive those banks and building societies that are repossessing homes – estimated to be up to 75,000 homes next year – and are being unsupportive of the public in need. When a building society sold someone's home for half price but then told them they still owed the difference it caused media outrage and was one reason why the Prime Minister, Gordon Brown, was trying to get the financial industries to behave more ethically.

Brands like Northern Rock and Bradford & Bingley are putting people before profits and are adopting a policy of waiting six months before repossessing any of their customers who fell into arrears. Northern Rock claimed it normally took 15 months to repossess a home and only as a last resort. Post recession the word 'repossession' will be the one word that judges all banks and building societies and will leave some brands damaged for generations. As a shareholder I wouldn't invest in any financial brand that is treating people badly unless you want to see your investment crash after the recession. And no amount of marketing budget will reverse public opinion.

SUMMARY

There's one rule and only one rule – be honest. If you lie it will catch you out. And remember, being 'economical with the truth' may work for a politician but the public won't buy it. You can't argue the case, because once you have been found out – your brand is dead. And the shareholders won't thank you. Trust is everything and once gone it's gone for good. The consumer has a lot of power, more than you because people will believe people first. And with the internet as a tool they can bring you down like David did Goliath.

8
SURVIVAL AND SECURITY

HOW ARE CONSUMERS RESPONDING TO THE RECESSION?

The 'credit crunch', a great example of rebranding a recession, hit the world in 2008 with far more of an impact than some first thought. Brands like Woolworth's and MFI have fallen with predictions of at least 10 major household brands failing in 2009.

A survey by the new community site, Ooffoo (part of the ethical retailer Natural Collection), revealed that 79% of respondents said the credit crunch did not affect their green or ethical considerations. With some pointing out that now more than ever, green and ethical factors should be supported, if they are to make it through the recession.

Although fast fashion will thrive in a recession, 12% of us are shopping more frequently for bargains at charity shops and other second-hand outlets. A friend of mine picked up a £400 designer dress for just £10, even Primark can't match that.

Allotments will be back in demand. Five years ago you had to wait up to two years for one in some areas. According to MINTEL, one in four adults are 'Good Lifers' embracing this thriftier way of living (even the young). Sixteen per cent of Brits say they are trying to be more self-sufficient in various ways, from growing their own vegetables to making their own clothes.

People have begun to rediscover home cooking again, with the abandonment of ready meals and the use of more raw ingredients. The losers seem to be those expensive boxed up organic vegetable deliveries. Consumer research from MINTEL over the last 12 months suggests that 41% of shoppers have switched to cheaper brands, and 34% have cut down on the premium ranges, such as Tesco Finest and Sainsbury's Taste the Difference.

There is now a noticeable shift away from premium, up market food, and luxurious ready meals and exotic produce. Two-thirds of us now look for the promotions and deals more often than we did a year ago with 29% of us spending more time comparing prices in the supermarket.

Staying at home will be the big change, which could be good as it'll re-establish the home as central to the family and social life. A third are already dining at home more rather than eating out, with one in five saying that they entertain friends at home more often than going out together to a restaurant. Bad news for Pret, as more than one in five people are now taking a packed lunch to work.

Discount brands like Lidl and Aldi have seen an increase in sales (Aldi had a 20% rise in a four week period, Iceland 15%), though new customers are still treating themselves to indulgences such as olives and good wine, according to a spokesman from Aldi. The losers are the big supermarkets. ONS figures in August 2008 showed that volume sales in the food retail market dropped for the first time.

ASDA has kept its focus on rolling back prices with its 50 p promotion and 2 p sausages. While Tesco, who pocket £1 for every £7 spent in the high street, launched an ultra-low-priced range called 'Market Value' and reduced prices to half on 3000 products. Sainsbury's launched its 'feed the family for a fiver' campaign and M&S created its dine in for £10. These market changes have forced many brands and retailers to refocus their marketing either onto price or value.

SELLING SURVIVAL AND SECURITY

In a period of national fear people change their values. Nothing makes us more sensitive to those close to us than the fear of them being hurt or killed. From storms and drought to terrorism, fear provides a great revelation of true values.

During comfortable periods we can adopt new values. It's all about Maslow's hierarchy. The basics – survival, warmth, food, water and security are animal fundamentals. But we live in a world, well most of us in the West at least, where these are sorted. I doubt anyone reading this book lives on the streets, so we can afford to adopt values. But we all adopt them in a different way. Some people adopt values as fashionable must haves, others as an accessory, and many as a personal statement – either positively or defensively. Some see it as essential lifestyle baggage. But for a few it marries to the basics of survival.

If environmentalism or people fall into the survival group then we sit up and listen. I often hear the phrase, 'why don't people get it? Can't they see what's happening?' The reality is that they do see it but it's like a movie. It doesn't touch them and more importantly it doesn't affect their sense of survival and security.

Fear is a powerful weapon in the ethical debate but only if you can really make people think and act. The trouble is, as I've learnt from the world of advertising, we have become immune to the horrors of the world. We eat our dinner on our laps watching starving kids on the news with (perhaps) just a momentary thought. We read fashion magazines parading the wares of our affluent and shallow society and within the pages is an article on poverty in the Third World. We live in a world where we are able to box off the uncomfortable truth.

The down side of fear is that it has a hierarchy. When terrorism is high on the agenda nobody is going to be asking if the security services are offsetting their carbon as they race around arresting people who are a threat to us.

In a period of recession there is a threat to our comfortable lifestyle. The man who was talking about changing his car for a new eco model is now just worried if he can afford to fill it up, or worse, stop it being repossessed. The Prius can wait till next year.

But ironically, less cash is good for the planet. We buy less so waste less (up to 25% of your shopping is wasted). We turn the lights off. We repair things that break rather than just DNU (dump 'n upgrade). We drive less. We don't throw old clothes away. We start to reuse and recycle things. We may even search the Freecycle website for people offering used items for free and even indulge in the odd dumpster diving with those barmy Freegans.

Freegans, now there's an interesting super green group. They were formed by a group of anti-capitalist vegans from New York in the 1990s. Refusing to support capitalism and therefore the exploitation of the world's resources and people, they decided to live off it for free by consuming what we waste. No one is sure if they are a movement, a political order or just a bunch of odd balls. It seems they make it up as they go along. Warren Oakes, a famous Freegan, described it as 'an anti-consumeristic ethic about eating'. He supports shoplifting and employee scams which is perhaps why the group have come in for more criticism than praise and have been branded as 'spongers' because they don't contribute to society. They've also been sent up on the radio by a comedian who spoofed a daily diary of a freegan, so perhaps in a small way they have added to society's joy.

In bad times we also retract to community. When times are tough we work together, share more and help those less fortunate. We all fall back on the old barter system of exchanging skills, tools and time. We actually become more sensitive to the plight of others because in the back of our head we are all scared that we will be the ones to fall. Community becomes important, the selfish individual less attractive.

For brands it's a good time to sell quality, because when the people are cash sensitive they either buy cheap or buy well. We live in a disposable society where longevity is no longer important. Even if it did last, we'd want to upgrade, to get the latest versions with all the latest gizmos. Just look at mobile phones. But now you think about buying a fridge, TV or washing machine that is reliable (no nasty repair bills) and lasts.

In a recession it's often thought that people go just for what's cheap, but this isn't true. People go for value. A cheap can of beans that tastes disgusting is not as good value as a good tin of bins that costs more. 'The sweet taste of low price soon wears off as the bitter taste of poor quality set in'. One of my first creative directors, Reg Starkey, had that pinned above his desk.

Ethics is a way to raise the value. It adds another layer that justifies a slightly higher price. Fairtrade baked beans vs normal ones, if the price is close guess who wins the sale? The trouble is, many ethical brands don't make ethics a real brand value, it's either a token badge or pitched as a guilt message, 'buy this or the starving kid gets it'.

A recession can do more to save the planet than any ad campaign, celebrity or green evangelists standing on street corners at the weekend. Who says politicians aren't taking the lead? Who says bankers are greedy bastards who don't give a damn about environmentalism? Between them they've started the biggest greening up movement in 90 years.

THE REAL COST OF LIVING

Both consumers and businesses are looking to survive, which means people are more focused on themselves than others or the environment..

When asked about the main responsibility of large companies, one third of Americans say companies should be competitive but not at the cost of reducing their green efforts. However, should a conflict arise between competitiveness and environmental protection, about half believe that protecting the environment is more important than economic growth. I can't see that going down well with the average board.

When I spoke to a building society recently the marketing manager was quite candid: 'half the board get it, they know they need to be greener and more ethical, the other half just want the money'.

Brands have a dilemma, they need to be more ruthless and sell harder but if they slip back to the old abusive ways it will come back to haunt them later. Banks and building societies that treat their customers badly during the recession will not be forgiven when times are good again and no amount of marketing will fix that. Consumers will abandon those brands en masse. It will be the fall after the recession. In this climate it's as much about preserving your income as preserving your brand reputation.

EDUCATION, EDUCATION, EDUCATION

If you add up all the green and ethical marketing it doesn't count for much compared to what is spent across the media board. The consumer gets a bit of the message but most are confused and unsure what to do or what responsibilities they have. A GfK Roper online survey (2000 American adults) suggested that almost half of Americans 'do not have the information to be personally involved in increasing their green behaviour' and 'aren't sure which products and packaging materials are recyclable'. Around half say they would do more for the environment if they only knew how and admit they know they should make the green lifestyle changes but are too busy, life is very demanding and green isn't top of the list.

There's a 'green gap' between consumer awareness and action. Consumers want to do the right thing but lack the information do so. They don't know how much of a positive effect they are making when buying different green products. It's too debatable, complicated and confusing; the companies who make being green easier and more affordable will be the winners.

Easy green or easy ethics is the best way to market behavioural change. And once people make physical changes the mind goes with them.

PARIS GOES ECO-ELECTRIC

Paris has made it very easy to be greener in your travels around the city. The 'Velib' bike sharing project has been so successful that they are now looking at an electric car-sharing system, dubbed 'Autolib'. The project would be a step forward towards promoting low-carbon urbanism.

The plan is to place 4000 electric cars around Paris and its outskirts for drivers in the programme to help themselves for short journeys. No need to buy an electric car, no hassle over recharging, maintenance or insurance, this is a good example of getting consumers to change their behavior the easy way. The next step would be conversion; users would start to look at owning their own electric car.

SUMMARY

Consumers' ethics change with the economic climate. When things get tough consumers change their ethical behaviour. In times of plenty it's easy to be high brow and evangelistic but when the credit crunch starts they adopt different values. Survival means that ethics come closer to home and family. In tough times people come before planet.

9
ENGAGING THE CONSUMER, SHARING RESPONSIBILITY

JUST DOING MY BIT

Probably one of the most common phrases I hear is 'I'm just doing my bit'. It's like a penance or your good deed for the day. Even the most cold hearted, money driven person needs to feel they are doing good at some point in the day. And if buying something fulfils this void that makes for easy emotional satisfaction.

AL GORE'S 'WE CAN SOLVE IT' CAMPAIGN

Ethical products in the environmental sector exploit this simple human need well. Changing the world or even saving it single handedly is beyond any of us. It's just too big and too complicated as Al Gore ('An Inconvenient Truth') says. But by marketing the 'one small step' approach people can get to grips with that. We have all been sold the unity approach; if all of us do a little bit we'll see a big change. Phrases around that thought are abundant in the world of green campaigning.

Gore has jumped on the same bandwagon of combined people power as Repower America with his 'we can solve it' campaign (the 'we' graphic is a 'me' upside down). The 'we' campaign is a project of The Alliance for Climate Protection and attempts to unify millions of Americans in order to change all of America's energy sources over to clean energy. This is ambitious but Gore is employing many marketing techniques to get his message across, backed by big budgets.

The 'do your bit' phrase has been used across a wide variety of campaigns from the government's energy saving campaign to PG Tips (pushing the Rainforest Alliance) and even a recycled toilet paper – 'Now doing your bit doesn't have to be a pain in the bum' (though Andrex was in fact the first to have FSC certification). It's fast becoming a cliché along with 'won't cost the earth'.

By attaching a simple promise that by buying this product or service you'll be 'doing your bit' adds emotional benefit. You are sharing responsibility without carrying the entire burden. It has a sense of community about it.

CHANGE THE WORLD FOR A FIVER

'We Are What We Do' is a global social change network that tries to inspire people to use their everyday actions to change the world. 'We Are What We Do' believes that if everyone makes a small change and does their bit it can actually amount to making a big difference. Their book 'How to Change the World for a Fiver,' was a big success – selling over 370 000 worldwide – and features 50 actions that anyone could do to help that don't require major change or sacrifice like 'turn off the water when you're brushing your teeth' or 'decline plastic bags whenever possible'. The ease and simplicity is part of the appeal. The book is beautifully illustrated and written, featuring contributions from many writers and art directors from the advertising and design industry.

The 'We Are What We Do' movement was started by a community worker who'd worked for 25 years for Community Links, David Robinson. Influenced by a marketing project by Nike, Robinson decided to create a social movement as a brand. Research by Interbrand identified three challenges:

1. Tell people what you want them to do (they need leadership) but keep it simple.
2. Tell people what can be achieved if lots of people did lots of little bits (as people think they can't make a difference alone).
3. Make it socially acceptable, part of anyone's lifestyle rather than just for people who go to church or are tree huggers.

It would also need to be engaging, quirky and cool – certainly something different. 'We Are What We Do' was born. Its first venture was the book, though the website has been the biggest influence.

Robinson is quoted in one interview as saying, 'Our mission was to inspire people to make simple adjustments to their day-to-day behaviour that, if enough of us did the same, would make a real difference'.

The movement has appealed to a broad range of organizations from schools to accountancy firms across almost 100 countries. Robinson was shocked by how quickly the word spread, 'We scatter a few seeds and they get taken by the wind. That is the nature of an idea like this. What's exciting is the very different kinds of people in all corners of the globe connecting with the idea'.

Robinson has discovered the power of an engaging idea. He could have set up just another worthy organization and published a worthy book but he raised the bar and got some of the best talent around to help and support him. The outcome was something different, engaging and highly appealing and he achieved what he set out to do – establish a brand. It seems odd that Nike, who have suffered criticism in the past for using child labour, should inspire an ethical movement. But then Nike is one of the best brands at marketing on the planet.

IT'S NOT WHAT YOU SAY BUT WHAT YOU DO

The Energy Saving Trust Green Barometer findings suggest that 80% of the population believe climate change is impacting upon us but 40% of the population are doing nothing about the environment. I would guess that of the 60% who are doing something, a percentage lie and many just recycle their rubbish. How many are really doing anything? The biggest problem groups like EST and the ACT ON campaign have is inspiring, motivating and incentivizing people to act. It's not enough just to say 'act now'.

Financial incentives certainly work, though the public are reluctant to pay more to save the planet. If you give them a discount or tax breaks you'll get motivation. The home energy audit promoted by the London Council and EST is a great idea but fails on the cost. Sure you may save a little money long term on reduced energy bills but not short term. This was always the problem selling double glazing, its payback was too long, most people bought it because it made the house look better (visual not numeric reasons). One of the problems with selling home energy audits is they cost around £200 for the survey and will land you with a bigger bill to sort out problems like windows, insulation or even a new boiler. As the credit crunch bites there's even less chance that a financially squeezed household will be sold on it. I think the average householder would love an audit and to make changes providing the government, who they hold in part to blame, pays for it.

A comment on a phone-in on the radio compared the environment to the economy: 'During the good times the City makes a fortune and reaps the benefit but in the bad times it's the public who pays. The environment has been abused by large corporations and governments for decades and now they want us to pay'.

Consumers in various surveys say they are willing to do their bit. But as I've said in another chapter, surveys make great numbers for PR but just how true are they? It's easy to say one thing but it's what you do that matters.

Ask people if they give to charity and almost all will say yes. But we all don't. Roger Moore, actor (James Bond) and a UNICEF ambassador since 1991 often shakes the collecting tin for 'Change for Good' on board flights. He recalls how everyone in economy gives, most in business but when you enter first class, everyone looks out of the window.

SUMMARY

The tradition of marketing is to talk at people but in the eco-ethical world marketing is often a waste of a good budget. People want to be engaged. By working together with the consumer you show genuine commitment as well as developing a relationship. The consumer really does want to be part of the solution and if you facilitate that they'll love you for it. It's all about shared responsibility.

10
FINDING
REASONS TO BUY

THE EMOTIONAL CONSUMER

The growing awareness and media coverage of environmental and ethical concerns means that people feel they should be making a more conscientious choice.

However, only a minority of people buy things purely on ethics. And few people are prepared to compromise product quality just to save the planet or support good causes. From a commercial point of view businesses need mass markets and mass markets buy on traditional values.

Looking at purchasing patterns, consumers are making emotional decisions based on perception, rather than necessarily having all the correct information; the consumer (and many green advocates) are poorly informed. Not surprising, when you consider that there seems to be a mass of so called facts, often with conflicting messages. And the media doesn't help either, by reporting issues poorly, by being played by different lobbies and by generally confusing their readers. As with most decision making, as politicians know all too well, people buy with their feelings rather than with logic. And when it's almost impossible to know what is right or wrong, they follow their instincts.

Understanding the difference between rational and emotional purchasing decisions and mindsets is critical to good marketing, especially in the field of ethics. The consumer buys with the heart before they buy with their head, even if they can rationalize it afterwards. If you doubt that, consider that three of the biggest purchases we make are recognized as being emotionally dominant – homes, cars and holidays. If you can sell those on emotions, you can sell anything. As one con man said on a TV documentary, 'if you want to get money out of people you won't do it with a logical argument, you need an emotional angle'.

THE R&E LINE – A SIMPLE MARKETING TOOL

A tool I use a great deal and one of the simplest and most useful marketing tools of all time is the rational to emotional line or the R&E line.

Polar tools are a very good way to simplify choices, simpler than the Boston Matrixes that often try to relate two issues, by contrast the R&E line is more single minded. It can be applied to many variants and has endless applications from single decision making to customer journeys. It's also a very useful tool for looking at pricing models. I find many marketing tools seek to complicate just so we can justify bigger fees or to try and confuse clients. Marketing isn't rocket science and the R&E line is so simple a child can use it.

An interesting factor in the correlation between pur-chasing mindsets and decision making is that in many cases the more rational a sell is the more it encourages people to 'think' logically and therefore make a more informed decision. The more emotive and/or impulsive, the quicker the decision is made. People just 'feel' they want it.

The other correlation is that cheap items tend to sit at the **R** end, premium at the **E** end. So if you want to improve your profits, reduce purchasing decision time, keep your pitch at the **E** end. Most added value is in the **E** section.

You can place a product, process, website, brand or even a retailer along the line. Once you know where it sits you can look at how to move it. If you look at the now demised Woolworth's its problem was obvious on the line. Emotionally it was an old friend but that didn't feature

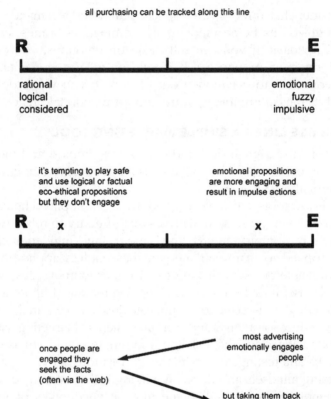

Figure 10.1 The R&E line

in the reasons to buy. Instead it sat at the **R** end – cheap and functional with little emotional reason to visit. By contrast Primark is cheap (and not perceived as an ethical retailer) but it sells fashion which is highly emotive. By contrast, online ethical retailers like Ethical Superstore, Natural Collections or Adili fall into the **E** section, fashion mixed with ethics, which allows them to charge a higher price.

The secret in using the R&E line is to isolate honestly those factors that contribute towards the sales along the line. I always find when doing this with clients in the Challenge Workshops which I run that they get a shock. Their idea is often way out with the facts, which is worrying if you are spending millions. However, it can identify very simply where they are going wrong and how to get their messaging right.

Take soap powder, probably one of the best examples of products that rely on added values, as they all pretty much do the same. Price, size, packaging type (does it fit in the cupboard) and product performance are generally rational. Smell, look, feel, brand image and reputation, packaging design and claims it makes you a better housewife are generally emotional.

Over the years brands have tried to up the sell on different rational and emotive aspects in order to give them an advantage and increase value perception; adding nice smells, offering liquids, powder and tablet variations and concentrates so as to reduce weight and storage. Doing emotive ad campaigns in order to make people feel good about the brand. Extra whiteness through the addition of chemicals that reflect UV light has been married with the emotional promise that a good housewife gets her family's clothes white (yep in these more enlightened days people still fall for it). Whiteness is rational, while being a better housewife is emotional. You can see how one can link to another on the line. The brands are constantly looking for a new promise and spin.

Now add to that ethics. Saving the environment, supporting charities that help people, reducing nasty chemicals in your clothes, reducing packaging to claim less damage to the environment are just as effective as selling points. All are highly emotive. It's no surprise that Aerial's 'turn to 30' campaign has been very successful. It's noticeable that all the supermarkets have launched own brand eco detergents, so they too believe there's a value in ethics in this area.

It may seem a bit pragmatic to position ethics just as an added emotional value when some people are so passionate about saving the planet. But the failure of many eco-ethical products is their inability to tune into the real world of marketing, which is why big brands that decide to offer ethical versions are a major threat to the small guys. You may well be a loyal Ecover buyer but if a more ethical detergent comes on the market at the same price would you stick with Ecover or switch to save the planet more? What if a well-known brand that you know cleans better launches an eco-ethical brand? P&G and Unilever have the technology, resources and marketing budget to launch probably the ultimate eco-ethical detergent at a more competitive price. Would you buy it?

THE CUSTOMER JOURNEY

We may well walk through the supermarket in a comatose state, like robots picking products off the shelves, but for other purchases there's a journey. That journey may well take us to one side of the R&E line and back. The way websites work means that they need to be mapped along an R&E line. Often people are drawn to them through an emotional appeal. Once there they are looking for information (rational). But the conversion to sale is often emotional, which is where many online sites fall down.

The overall aim of the R&E line is to get to the **E** side. Think **E** not just for emotions but ethics.

NLP – THE AARDVARK TOOL

About five years ago I was introduced to NLP through both my brother Paul and another Paul, at a leading firm of managing consultants. My brother had got into it through training while the other Paul had developed it into a sales tool. I developed a tool called **A**ard**V**ar**K** that uses the **A**,

V, **K** aspects of NLP. The first time we used it was to help The Stroke Association pitch for charity of the year for BAe. They won. A year later we helped Age Concern take on Macmillan (sadly they lost that time, cancer is a more powerful appeal than age, but even getting short listed was a surprise for them).

I won't do a history of NLP but Neuro-linguistic programming has become very popular and crosses many areas from life coaching, training, management to sales and marketing (though it's yet to make an impact in advertising circles). It's been adapted into many forms, though bastardized may be a better description. However, one of its more useful factors is the understanding of three primary mindsets, the **A**, **V** and **K**. It explains much about why people think the way they do and why a lot of straight and dull marketing doesn't work.

A mindsets are very logical, anal and analytical – your typical finance director, banker, statistician and programmer. Their thinking is very linear and unemotional. They buy on reason and logic, being able to pre-rationalize a purchase. They are usually the last people to be able to understand consumers and marketing yet they tend to control the budgets. Because they think logically they often make the mistake of thinking that everyone thinks logically. I've come across a good few MDs with a financial background who meddle in marketing and think mistakenly that all advertising has to do is tell it as it is. Unfortunately **A** mindsets are rarely open minded so are hard to challenge.

V are what most of us are, visual mindsets. Hence why we all dress differently, like different clothes, colours and designs. The relationship between the eye and mind is very strong. Without the **V** mindset we'd have no fashion, art, beauty, photography or design. Life would be very grey. We'd all be happy wearing the same clothes and looking like clones.

K (kinaesthetic) are all about feelings and emotions, again something most of us respond to. They feel the world, they are touched and sensitive. They experience life through emotions.

Now there are very few people who are solely one type and all of us have a mix that can vary. If we are filling out a tax form most of us will be in an **A** mindset. If we are at the cinema we are in a **V** with some **K**. In love, pure **K**. But we all know people who would have a bias towards one type.

It goes a little way towards explaining why research and surveys can be very misleading. When asked to fill out forms or respond to questions like 'what do you think of…' people respond in **A** mindsets. Getting consumers to be honest requires asking them how they 'feel' or 'see'.

If you ask three people with these different mindsets to describe a café, for example, they'd all give you a different perspective on it. You may well think they are talking about three different cafes. The **A** mindset would talk about size, pricing, numbers of tables and chairs and sound. The **V** mindset would describe the look of the place and refer to the designer cups and colours. The **K** mindset would tell how they feel in the place, relaxed, at one and how they love it. Each would use words that fit their mindsets. Visual people use a lot of visual words like 'look' and 'see'.

Referring to the closure of Woolworth's, I listened to several conversations, each one different. One person said: 'have you heard Woollies are closing?' (**A**); another 'I see Woolworth's are closing' (**V**); and 'isn't it a shame, I feel we are losing a bit of our heritage' (**K**).

NLP purists may well see this as adaptation of NLP but it highlights different consumer types and if it makes us think more about how we communicate it will help us produce more effective communication.

By using the three different languages of **A**, **V** and **K** you can increase the appeal of your message. **A** mindsets don't respond to visualization, so use facts. Advertising copy can be more effective if it combines a mix of words that communicates with all types. It's also important to use strong images as most people are visual and convey emotions, but please avoid clichés – green landscapes, smiling people, flowers, wind turbines and butterflies are signs of insincerity as consumers know you've taken them from a picture library and are faking it. People want real images, not icons.

SIMPLIFYING CONSUMER CHOICE – THE POWER OF THREE

The method of three is a very useful approach. Try and keep all choices to three. And then the next choice to three. It's a technique that works on all levels and works in line with how we think. It's especially useful with websites.

When I worked with the National Blood Service to redesign their website I divided it into three entry points. We used the Science Museum as visual example. You have the serious stuff (Alpha zone) up top for the professionals – doctors, blood experts and medical researchers and students. The Launch Pad is a playful (Beta zone) place, where education is made fun. The rest of the museum is explorative. We created three entry buttons, one for medics, one for kids and one for donors. It's a simple architecture compared to so many websites that resemble the Hampton Court maze.

We created a visual graphic – a blood barometer (a test tube) to visualize blood levels in the blood bank. It was never too full or too empty. It just went up and down to make people see how its resources fluctuated (remember what I said about NLP?).

For the kids we developed a fun and interactive site. We signed up Nick Arnold (no relation) who'd done the Horrible Science books. We also designed an interactive game based on the cult 60s film 'Fantastic Voyage'. In the film a diplomat is nearly assassinated and lies in a critical state. To save him a submarine is shrunk to microscopic size and injected into his blood stream with a small crew featuring Raquel Welch, Donald Pleasence and Stephen Boyd. In the game, as you travelled around you'd collect blood points (pints) over time, whilst you stopped to read about organs and information on the body. But at an unpredictable point there'd be an accident, 'you've been run over, 15 pints needed'. If you haven't enough, you're dead. Good way to make kids think about how blood is used in operations and emergencies. Sadly, owing to limited funds the game didn't happen.

For the donor there were maps of local collection points and information about where the blood goes. When working on the site we watched Tony Hancock's brilliant 'Blood Donor' comedy sketch many times (which was also planned to appear on the site). Hancock captures the typical consumer's attitude about blood, once they've given it they want to know what's happening to it. This is why the TV campaign for blood donation has been so successful; it tells you that your blood could be the pint that saves a life. In reality it goes into the system and that's it. But giving blood is something we do because we all like to do good. We get a great sense of satisfaction and it's worth knowing that in a small way we may have saved a life.

The British Blood Service has been very clever in using good marketing to get donors while other countries resort to paying for blood donations. When you reduce things to money, and it's one of the lowest values you can use, people behave differently. When you position something as helping mankind it attracts people who care, which most of us do. Some people have even been caught using false names so they can donate more often.

The Blood Service website has gone through a number of changes over the years but it's kept the combination of fun and facts – a good example of NLP art work – and is a good example of balancing rational and emotional values.

PEOPLE vs PLANET – THE GEOGRAPHY OF NEEDS

As mentioned in other parts of this book, you have to consider the difference between people and planet issues. Consumers are drawn towards people issues more than the planet, that is not to say people aren't concerned with the planet but when forced to make a choice the majority go for people. This has been supported by a number of surveys, several I've conducted and by the popularity of Fairtrade.

When we held the People vs Planet debate in London our online survey (and this was targeted at ethically aware people) the vast majority opted for people. However, the planet lobby has been very successful in making everyone think we are only really concerned with the environment. Interestingly, when people see how the environment affects people – something the Christian Aid ads did well – they do respond.

Figure 10.2 shows how people start from self (me), spread to family and community and only then to planet. We are programmed to protect ourselves and others close to us. Community can be defined in many ways – the people we live with, shared interests, even country.

What is interesting is how people see the problem. People we feel we're responsible for and can make a difference to but the planet, well we feel the blame lies more with governments and corporations, oil companies especially. People feel that these people need to take responsibility and sort out the mess not pass it onto the public. Where they can they will do something but it's a gigantic problem that they want big people to sort out. It's like asking people to support a local cause, most people would have no problem fund raising via a fun run, swim or bike

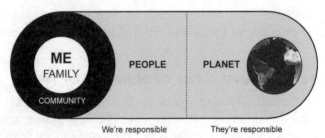

We're responsible   They're responsible

Figure 10.2 Geography of needs

ride. But would you do the same for the NHS? Most of us would look at the government and demand they sort it out. Sadly most research also reveals that people feel governments show little or no leadership in solving world problems and many feel they are bullied and pressured by large greedy companies to bend the rules.

In one survey we conducted 59% of consumers felt that governments and corporations were responsible for sorting out planet issues. In the Havas Global study, only 11% of consumers felt governments were doing enough. Damning statistics.

SUMMARY

Understanding consumers isn't just about going through lots of research data, people aren't mice. It's about understanding the psychology of behaviour. What makes people tick. The differences between emotional and rational mindsets and where your marketing sits within them and how it responds to them. Most importantly, don't just badge people up, especially into groups like A, B, C1 – these people don't exist except in the lazy imagination of those in ivory towers. There are many models out there that can be adapted in order to help us understand consumers. There are also some simple common sense ones – like keep it simple.

11
RESEARCH AND SURVEYS

THE NUMERIC SOCIETY

Numbers are very two dimensional, prone to misconception and on their own tell us little. Can we really get meaning from them? Knowing the coordinates of a town means nothing, but put them into Google Earth and suddenly you have another dimension. Go there and you'll really know.

Few of us have probably thought about it, but we now live in a 'numeric society'. Everything is measured, evaluated and judged on numbers. Our governments don't see the problem they see a statistic. They don't see real solutions but numbers. If they can make the numbers fit then problem solved.

Education, health and now the environment is all about numbers. Percentages, targets, tonnes, everything has a numeric value. The trouble is we all know it's not about numbers. Human psychology, human passion, social trends and concern for people and the planet are not measurable. It's like looking at a sheet of music rather than listening to it being played – big difference. But the real danger with this approach is that it's two dimensional and doesn't reflect reality. When you only see the world as numbers you start to make mistakes. There's a great quote, I think Ogilvy said it: 'too many people use statistics like a drunk uses a lamp post, for support rather than illumination'.

NEW IDEAS IN PROFILING

I make no apologies about my damnation of A, B, C1 as the most ridiculous and unscientific approach to defining consumers. Many planners I know feel the same. You really couldn't invent a more ludicrous methodology. It is another numeric based definition that has little connection with reality. I once suggested to a client that we use a new system that defines consumers by 12 types. Each type was defined by characteristics and personality and we could even predict their behaviour on both a monthly and almost daily basis. The client was gripped. Having obtained his birthday from his PA, I went on to define him using this new methodology. He was stunned. 'What's it called', he asked excitedly. 'Astrology', I replied. At least he saw the funny side of it although he had to agree that it was actually a better mythology than many that are used.

NLP AND ENNEAGRAMS

Two other approaches which I've used in defining consumers are NLP (see above) and enneagrams. Enneagrams is a very old psychology profiling system dating back to the Greeks. It has nine types and is surprisingly accurate; almost everyone fits into one section. What makes it more relevant to marketing is that it's based on emotional and not rational behaviour, and not on wealth, job type, class or even when you were born! The belief behind it is that it is the emotional part of us that drives us towards certain behaviour, jobs, lifestyle and even wealth, or lack of it. And relevant to us marketing folk, what brands and products we buy.

Helpers for example, tend to get an emotional reward from helping others. It comes as no surprise that they are less obsessed with materialism and money, and so opt for helper roles in society (social workers, nurses, teachers and many other low paid jobs). Low paid because history has shown that these people are not driven by money and so don't demand it.

Achievers, by contrast, seek all those things that make them look successful. They buy brands that make statements about themselves and advertise their achievements. Deep down, emotionally they are very insecure and fear failure, which is what drives them to be successful. Achievers are also opportunists. Take them to a party and they're there to network, meanwhile the helper is helping wash the dishes.

There are seven other types and an extra dimension to each type called wings. I won't go into these in detail, that'd be a book in itself, but look up enneagrams on the web (you can do a test at www.enneagraminstitute.com, click on Free RHETI Sampler). There's also a great book on it called 'The Enneagram Made Easy: Discover the 9 Types of People', by Renee Baron and Elizabeth Wagele.

EMOTIVATIONS

Working with a life coaching company called Finding Clarity, who introduced me to enneagrams, I adapted them into a marketing tool called Emotivations. We were then working with More Than insurance and introduced them to the concept of enneagrams. Most of the marketing department were very enthusiastic about it and did the profile. Most turned out to be loyalists.

The tool became very useful in looking at issues of member get member (also called friend get friend or refer a friend). We looked at the typical More Than customer as against the nine types. Half we dismissed – achievers, for example, like fast flash cars and are unlikely to be More Than customers (MT prefer older, sensible drivers, like Volvo owners who don't have accidents and have drives in front of their houses). Of the nine groups several stood out as the type that, as a loyal customer, would be worth targeting.

To give a top line summary (though I recommend you read the book on it), the nine types are:

REFORMERS are one of the strongest ethical groups, driven by the need to do good and what's right. They have strong principles and values, usually idealistic. They want to convert people and are strong advocates of things they think are good. They are your typical environmental champion.

HELPERS are caring, selfless, interpersonal, generous and will go out of their way for others. They are non materialistic and not driven by money. They are charitable and happy to go out at the weekend and help clean up an environmental space, but are strong on people ethics such as fair trade. They support charitable and ethical causes but don't have a lot of money so can't afford to buy over priced ethical products in the supermarket.

ACHIEVERS are success-oriented, pragmatic and highly driven, professional and image-conscious. Deep down they fear failure. Materialistic, money and reward orientated, they seek recognition. Ethics for them is a vehicle, good for dinner parties, corporate conversations, golf chat or looking cool and caring. As an image they follow it because the people who matter are into it, these people like to follow up market trends. Only rarely does one care and use their drive to make things happen and become a green champion.

INDIVIDUALISTS are very private and sensitive, withdrawn, expressive, dramatic, self-absorbed, often temperamental and moody. They can have low self esteem so don't buy brands that say 'look at me' though they may opt for the alternative brand in order to show their rejection of the masses. They are likely to be early cause campaigners but as soon as the masses adopt the cause they move on. They are early greens who have now found a new cause. They can be selfish and the very opposite of helpers: 'Sort your own problems out, I've enough of my own'. They are hard to sell to unless you're a unique or black spot brand. They will buy local if everyone else is buying in supermarkets. They bought organic before it became trendy; probably grow their own veg.

INVESTIGATORS are intense, curious, self improving, innovative, secretive, isolated but perceptive. They like a good book rather than a night out in the Hope and Anchor. They seek to be experts, offering advice which they usually take a lot of trouble and care to get right. Knowledge is an attraction to them. They respect expertise and hate sloppiness and vagueness. They know their stuff when it comes to ethics. They don't waste your time arguing but can also be very narrow minded once they have become fixed on a belief, adjusting facts and the world to fit that belief.

LOYALISTS are committed, hard working and as their name implies, they become loyal to beliefs and associations –

good if they buy your brand or follow an ethical belief. If they buy your brand for an ethical reason they stick with it, it'll take a lot to break the bond. Emotionally they are security orientated; they like conformity and are suspicious of change. They like the comfort of knowing where they stand and hate uncertainty. They like to work in insurance companies!

ENTHUSIASTS live life to the full, seeking the stimulation of adventure and activity. They are always busy, juggling a million things, rushing from here to there, chaotic but very versatile. Extrovert, they are fun loving and would get bored if they had nothing to do. They always say yes to another activity, doing things seems to be their passion and they love to be involved. Once they get into something they are very passionate about it. The busy hippie types and the environmental adventurers fit into this group. If you want anyone to organize an event they are first in the queue. Ethically they get involved and are very active – the type handing out leaflets against animal testing on a Saturday morning in the high street.

CHALLENGERS are control freaks who are scared of not being in control. Self confident, decisive and dominating, they like to be the boss and they are always right. They can be confrontational and don't like being told what to do. Critical, often to reinforce their superiority, they can be very argumentative. They have to be the expert and value their own opinion above others. Once they think they know better they will try and convince others. You've probably met the type either side of the argument 'is man to blame for global warming?' Give them a platform and they lecture for hours. Good to have on your side if you're championing an ethical cause.

PEACEMAKERS are agreeable, easy going, the very opposite of challengers. They sit on the fence and follow
the crowd, rather than expressing a personal choice. Self-
effacing, they are good listeners and very aware. They
rarely challenge or stand up alone. Instead they go with
the flow and so buy in tune with the masses. These types
champion love and peace in the world, hate confrontation
and war or exploitation, especially of people. Community
is very important so they will buy local and support people-
based ethics such as fair trade.

When you apply these types to a member get member
campaign, you can see how some types are better than
others. This is just a top line assessment but it gives you
an idea.

- **Reformers** would recommend you if they thought you
  were good and right, but insurance is low priority. If it
  was insurance that was saving the planet they'd be your
  biggest advocate.
- **Helpers** like to help each other so recommending More
  Than could be positioned as saving a friend time and
  money and helping them not pick the wrong company.
  When appealing to them you need to address what's in
  it for their friends.
- **Achievers** would lecture people on the fact that their
  insurance company is best if they thought it looked good,
  though it's not a high priority in their life.
- **Individualists** would think that people should do
  their own problem solving: 'I spent hours sorting out my
  insurance, why should I help you sort out yours?'
- **Investigators** check things out so if they have selected
  you as their insurance company they feel it's the best
  choice; they see themselves as wise so why not advise
  others? You need to flatter their ego and make them feel
  valuable.

- **Loyalists** are very supportive and do what you ask out of loyalty. They will form strong relationships with brands (the type who always buys a Volvo) so why not share those values with loyal friends?
- **Enthusiasts** never say no. Make it fun and challenging and they'll be off telling everyone. The only problem is they're so busy they may never get around to actually telling anyone.
- **Challengers** are aggressive and hate being used. Forget it.
- **Peacemakers** are too complacent to be good advocates. But as good communicators and listeners they are social creatures who, if they are convinced, may act as a linker for you.

One common technique used for MGM campaigns is the 'recommend a friend and we'll give you a £25 M&S voucher'. When is it an incentive or a bribe? When is an offer corrupting your values and using you? Do people feel rewarded or feel they have sold out? Different types respond differently to a £25 voucher. You can't make the assumption that people are all the same.

Why not try offering the voucher to the friend – helpers would love that. Or share it, peacemakers would love that. Or give it to a good cause, reformers and enthusiasts would love that.

VISUALITY PROFILING OVER NUMERIC

Rather than look at a numeric measure why not adopt a visual one (if you've read the section on NLP, this is the **V** bit of AVK).

Recently we've been looking at profiling people through visual definitions – colours, patterns, even choice of furniture or a cup design. Why not? If you are selling fashion the only numbers that are of value are the dress size and price. People buy on looks so why not profile them that way? I believe that having been engrossed in numeric evaluation for too many decades the marketing industry will wake up to the fact that people aren't numbers and will look at more imaginative and innovative approaches to measurement and evaluation.

For a recent online ethical fashion client we proposed setting up a series of wardrobes. Customers are encouraged to pick one from a range. Each one in a very different style: traditional, classic, modern, retro, futuristic, simple, etc. The customer is then asked to pick a different interior finish (plain, textured, patterned) and finally a colour. The wardrobe not only defines them but becomes their identity; within it, their buying history, wish list and suggestions from the brand. 'Dear customer, we've put something special in your wardrobe...'. Because online retailers can't offer the shopping experience you get with real shops, it helps make the site more alive and engaging. The idea then extends to a road show – a series of wardrobes touring shopping centres and exhibitions, each one transformed into a magical display of ethical designer clothes.

If you stand at the entrance of any store even the non expert can make a judgement based on how people look. You don't need numbers, just instinct. I strongly recommend that in the world of ethics number can easily take you down the wrong path. Especially when so many are dubious.

JOEL MAKOWER, THE GREEN BLOGGER ON RESEARCH

One of my favourite bloggers is Joel Makower; a great writer, he highlights some interesting insights from research on his site. To quote Joel directly from his site, 'I've seen enough research data on Americans' green buying habits over nearly twenty years that I've become immune to much of it. It's not that I think such research is shoddy; it's just that I've found consumers' credibility on the issue wanting'. As Joel points out, what people say and what they do are usually the opposite, consumer behaviour proves it.

In one survey on fair trade we were given by a client, 71% of people said they buy it, yet sales suggested that just 17% did. The consumer can't be trusted to tell the truth. However, at least it suggests that the intent is there.

I have mixed feelings about research; like Makower, I love it when it's right but feel that too often it's inaccurate and/or used badly. Several years ago I was the keynote speaker at the Business Intelligence Group's annual conference (BIG). I spoke to many attendees and the conclusion was that most businesses use research to cover their own backsides and not to gain valuable insight to help them make informed decisions. Great research is gold to creative people and strategists. But bad research is destructive and can do permanent damage to a brand.

In the word of ethics and eco-ethical marketing you can find a survey that will support any point of view or worse, twist results. The GfK Roper Green Gauge survey tracks Americans' green buying habits; the environmental attitudes and belief systems of five market segmentations of American consumers. In one report it claimed, 'nearly nine in ten Americans say they are fretting over the fate of the earth!' Makower is not just a good blogger but a good digger, he rang them up and dug deeper. It turns out the figure is a bit of exaggeration, in fact just 41% were serious about being seriously concerned about the environment.

The report also highlights that when consumers are looking for information on a company's environmental practices and CSR policies, they don't look on the website. Really? Their findings were that they use traditional media

– TV programmes 59%, newspaper articles 49%, online articles 39% and friends, family, and people you know 34%.

Consumers do seem to believe packaging and labels, something we also found out in the Ethical Shopping Survey. If the label says it's biodegradable, organic or natural, the consumer has a level of trust with that message. Although 55% believe many environmentally safe products are not better for the environment.

The report also states that 74% of consumers believe greener products are too expensive, while 61% say they don't work as well. Sadly, there is a truth in this claim as anyone who buys lots of ethical products knows.

If you read numerous reports you could be left very confused. One will tell you that the environment is all that matters, for example 56% of Americans are worried about the destruction of the rainforest, yet drive big gas guzzling cars. Another will tell you that we care about people more. My advice; ignore other people's surveys and do your own. Which is what I did.

'ANTI-MARKETING'

The Local Government Association found that a great deal of packaging in supermarkets was not recyclable. The LGA bought 29 products from various stores and found that the best performers were local markets (76%) and then local shops (74%). The best supermarket was Sainsbury's at 70%, Asda (69%), Morrison's (67%) and Tesco (65%). Worse were Lidl and surprisingly M&S with just 62%. Not surprisingly, M&S get beaten up in the press (so much for Plan A) and Sainsbury's get a medal.

This is not untypical of the kind of surveys doing the rounds. But let's look at this survey a bit closer. Just taking 29 products when a supermarket like M&S stocks 5500 or the major brands over 20 000; that's less than 0.5%

of M&S's stock and an even smaller fraction of Tesco's. Any statistician would allow for a margin of difference, say 10%. The difference between the best and worse is just 8%. It hardly defines a difference between a good shop and a bad one. This survey is grossly unscientific and irresponsible at best. But these surveys find themselves into the press and act as 'anti-marketing', damaging some brands' hard earned image and inflating others. Sadly, consumers rarely look behind the statistics and tend to believe anything reported in the press. You can understand why some brands think it's easier not to venture into the ethical space.

BEWARE OF THE NUMBERS

A survey sample of 1000 people used to be the basic minimum if you wanted any newspaper to take you seriously and cover your outcomes. But recently almost any number will do. One survey revealed that using celebrities in TV ads was less effective than using ordinary people. Now I'm not a great fan of using celebs but in marketing terms the right one can perform miracles for sales. The survey was carried out among 62 students in a university cafeteria. You can see the danger of rubbish like this, people read the headline, another marketing myth is added to the big pile and decisions are made down the line based on a mistruth.

NEVER TRUST SURVEYS UNLESS YOU'VE ASKED THE THREE GOLDEN QUESTIONS

The first question is **how many people and what percentage do they represent?** Sixty-two people even as a percentage of students is not enough to have a valid outcome. Even 1000 is a small number when you consider there are over 56 million people in the UK. Twenty-nine products against 5500 is a joke.

The second question is **where was it asked?** Geographical location can give you very different results. For example, one carpet maker we pitched for, Brintons, did a survey and discovered that up North people prefer patterned carpets and down South they prefer plain. Had the survey only been carried out in one area the result would have been biased. If you are surveying people outside supermarkets, that's great for asking them about food shopping habits or the cost of bread but not a great place to ask about sex, cars or politics – wrong frame of mind.

There's also a big difference between street and online. I don't rate online surveys as it's often too easy to just tick anything and if they are long or complicated they only attract certain types. If people are paid to fill them in, can you trust them? Housewives, small businessmen and creative types just aren't interested or are too busy. So who does? Maybe sad single geeks who play 'World of Warcraft' and need pocket money. If you doubt that people tell lies online, go to any dating site and then arrange a meeting. Then play spot the massive difference.

I came across one survey on a business site for time management that took too long, and was a bit pointless, as their results wouldn't have reflected that of busy people.

Telephone interviews also concern me as they are limited to people who are at home and are probably single – who else would talk to a phone researcher? Having taken part in several (driven by curiosity) it was easy to lie and I felt the need to project my self image as I want to be seen as successful and great, rather than the less glamorous truth. How many of us have lied about our incomes and gone for a higher value?

The third question is **what were the questions?** Simple words like 'think' and 'feel' can generate very different answers. Anyone who has studied NLP will tell you just how important words are in manipulating mindsets. You can also write a question two ways, it's easier to get people to agree than disagree. Multiple choice as a technique also limits the answers and often includes an option that allows you to opt out while being seen to answer the question (few of us like to seem uncooperative). Suddenly all those moderate voters are included in the 'most people think...' press release.

Always look for the hidden agenda? Brands like surveys that make their product look good, especially within the ethical arena – 67% of people think Product X is better for the environment than Products Y and Z. Green groups (charities and NGOs) like to use them to attack corporations. Local authorities and politicians use them to justify their actions. As they say, there are 'truths, lies and statistics'.

There are those that will load the question in order to get the result that justifies the agenda of the client. When Islington council were planning to put in speed bumps they conducted a survey of residents that (surprisingly) gave them the evidence they needed but it was later revealed that the questions were loaded and twisted to justify their decision. Asking if you 'want safer roads' isn't the same as asking 'do you want speed bumps?' when there are many other options. Or justifying new laws that take away your liberty by asking 'would you like a world of peace, free from terror?' Using predictable 'yes' answer style questions is an old trick.

I'm not saying all surveys are dubious but there are many that are. It's important that any decision you make, especially when it involves a marketing budget, should be informed and from a point of knowledge – not assumptions, hearsay, myths or worse, false evidence.

That may seem common sense, but common sense is rarely common.

THE ETHICAL SHOPPING SURVEY

It took a year of facing cynics but we finally carried out the Ethical Shopping Survey in 2008. We approached it differently, instead of asking people what they thought we asked them to put a price on it. That simple change in approach seems to get a more honest answer because it forces people to value things.

We wanted to know if people really were prepared to pay more for ethical goods and if so, which ethics were more important than others. After much investigation we found one product that was ideal. The product was seen as functional (so not too many emotional values at play, allowing us to see how the emotions of an ethical value added to it) and only cost £1. Because we were asking people how much extra they'd pay, £1 was a simple figure for consumers to work with. The product? A twin pack of toilet rolls.

Steve Phillips, who founded one of the more innovative research companies, Spring, recommended we first try the survey out on a bus. I wonder how many companies have done that? I do recommend it. The first thing you discover is just how middle class and university educated you are. Ordinary people don't understand your language or what you think you mean. We conducted 200 surveys on buses and tuned many of the questions and the language. We also introduced a narrative section for the agents to fill in – essential in order to get a third dimension on the survey. This was later to prove to be very valuable.

We conducted 1200 surveys across the whole UK (major cities – Leeds, Manchester, Birmingham, London, etc). Sol Wei, my assistant, did a great job recruiting (mostly psychology) students from universities to act as agents.

We first asked people where they shopped. We wanted to position the toilet roll and the ethical options in familiar territory and as their supermarket's own label brand. This makes it more comfortable.

We then asked people to nominate an extra amount above £1 they'd pay (or not) to buy a more ethical option. We used the term 'if it was badged...' for several types as this seemed to help people understand the concept better (one benefit of the bus test).The options we tested were:

- Organic;
- fair trade;
- locally produced;
- made from recycled paper;
- low carbon footprint;
- environmentally friendly;
- a percentage of profits went to a worthwhile charity;
- no animal was harmed making this product.

We then asked who they thought was responsible for saving the planet. And finally, if they recognized the symbols for recycled, organic and Fairtrade.

The results were very interesting, though I should add that I would not go as far to say that this represents the thoughts of all UK shoppers. Seventy-nine per cent of those questioned shopped at either Tesco (34%), Sainsbury's (27%) or ASDA (18%). Morrison's came in at 5%, Waitrose 4%, the Co-op 4% and others 8%. Seventy-four per cent were women, 26% men. The Co-op is the number one ethical supermarket. Had we interviewed only their customers we may have seen a slightly different result.

What the numbers revealed was interesting but what the narrative revealed, I found even more interesting. Take animal testing. Few people will pay extra for it. What does that tell you? People don't care. Wrong. The narrative adds another dimension. People won't pay extra because they think it should be a moral basic that companies don't test on animals and they don't believe the public should pay a premium for it. You can see how numbers alone can be deceptive.

Environmental issues like 'low carbon footprint' and 'environmentally friendly' didn't score as well as people-based ethics. The narrative revealed that people don't understand what a carbon footprint is and people don't believe terms like 'environmentally friendly' thinking it was just greenwash: 'How come something I was buying yesterday is suddenly saving the planet? It's a con'.

But people do get Fairtrade, in fact 78% of shoppers recognized the symbol. Organic seemed to depend upon how people saw it. Some people see organic as a price con: 'It's just an excuse to charge you extra for the same stuff'. There is a difference between two types of purchasers. Those that see it from a green angle and those who see it as a quality product that tastes better. Less than a third recognized the Soil Association's organic symbol, which is perhaps not surprising, considering how badly and blandly designed it is. The Tesco organic symbol is far more recognizable.

'Made from recycled paper' raised the issue of 'isn't toilet paper made from recycled paper anyway?' There is an association with recycled paper making products cheaper and therefore there's a reluctance to pay extra, but recycling was seen as a positive act. The recycled symbol was recognized by 91% of shoppers, though people are confused by the number of different symbols.

Local was a popular choice as it was seen as supporting the community; however, slightly more popular was supporting a worthwhile charity.

Overall, Fairtrade came out on top and donating to charities second. In the battle between people and planet, people won.

And were shoppers prepared to pay more? Yes, on average up to 19% more because they see ethical values as added value. But they won't pay to correct other people's mistakes.

A recent survey by TNS claims that Americans would pay more for green products (well that's what 53% of US consumers say). But those of us who work in the ethical marketing arena know there's a big difference between the talk and the walk. Only 19% were genuinely concerned with a company's greenness.

Another survey carried out in Europe for a major shoe brand was equally revealing. Woman who claimed to be highly interested in buying ethical shoes ended up opting for fashion first. By contrast men were more inclined to buy ethical footwear than they claimed in the survey. The challenge is for brands to convert the intent into action.

Marketing ethics is equally as revealing when you ask people about green ads. The Burst Media online survey in the US looked at consumers' response to green ads. Seventy per cent recalled seeing green ads occasionally, 20% 'never' believe the claims and 66% only believed the claims 'sometimes', leaving just 14% who actually trust green ads (less than the 17% who trust ads at all). It seems that you're better off not marketing green according to this survey.

The Havas Media Global Study reveals that 35% of shoppers are prepared to pay more for ethical goods, interesting but which ethics? Mintel, Chicago, found that nearly 200 million Americans are now actively purchasing green products, an impressive number. In the UK, despite an estimated £250m being spent on 'green marketing', Lippincott found that 70% of UK consumers couldn't name a single brand taking a lead on climate change.

WHO'S TO BLAME AND WHO'S GOING TO FIX IT?

There's a real lack of leadership from politicians on ethics, especially where environmental issues are concerned. When politicians are too busy fighting wars over oil and invading other countries it's hard to become an ethical leader. Well that's how many greens see it. The Havas Media study also reveals that 89% of people don't feel that governments are doing enough.

In our shopping survey we asked the big question, 'who do you think should be responsible for saving the planet?'

Thirty-two per cent believed the government should be responsible; 23% believed big brands, 19% believed retailers, 26% believed the consumer, which means 42% believed that businesses should be responsible. People feel that it's the responsibility of governments and big corporations to take leadership: 'They got us in this mess; they should get us out of it.'. 'Governments have allowed big companies to rape the planet, why should we be responsible?' The planet is a big issue and demands that governments sort it out.

A Channel 4 survey (2005) asked 'Who should be responsible for tackling Climate Change?' The answers given were:

- Government   79%
- World leaders   75%
- People   74%
- Business   68%
- Local councils   62%

Slightly more worrying survey results come from Vizu Corp. and Green Home. The poll found a growing divide in how the public react to global warming. Nearly one third indicated that they would not change their behaviour and around a fifth claimed that they are doing everything they can. As a reflection of the trend of environmentalism, 61% expect the topic to fade with the next major media story.

CHANGING CONSUMER HABITS

Despite millions being spent on ACT TOGETHER campaigns, consumers keep saying one thing and doing another. Intent is great but you need action. The credit crunch has forced change, though it's money that is driving it not ethics. We drive less in order to save money on petrol. We waste less because we buy less, to save money. We reuse and recycle rather than replace, to save money. Strangely, a recession is the first thing that has really made a difference. Bet no one thought that up as a marketing technique in any of those government think tanks.

A BBC research online poll of 21 000 people across 21 countries suggested that 70% of people said they were prepared to change their lifestyle in order to address climate change and 50% favoured increased taxes on fossil fuels. This I really doubt, given the uproar over recent fuel price increases, and what defines 'changing their lifestyle'. This is a good example of fluffy research that's probably more about intent than genuine action.

A quote I picked up from Joel's site seems to capture it well: 'Most people are doing something, though the majority are engaging in "Random Acts of Greenness" – a few tweaks to their products, facilities, policies, or practices, but nothing that could be construed as systemic change'.

SUMMARY

To use an old quote, 'many people use research like a drunk uses a lamp post, to prop themselves up rather than for illumination'. The message here is that when used properly research can be very illuminating but it can only be a guideline and I'd always consider instinct and experience to be superior. Sometimes you just know what's right.

I've always disagreed that you can test executions because ads work within an emotional context so when you ask people what they think you get a rational answer. Using research for intelligent guidance is good, but using it to justify a bad decision or to cover one's backside is too often the case.

And finally people are not numbers or letters. If you think of people that way you are not a marketing person but an accountant.

12
THE BUSINESS AND
RELIGION OF ETHICS

ETHICS AS A RELIGION

Despite the UK losing its religion (though 70% of the UK population are classed as Christians) and considering that few of us go to church, the average person still upholds basic social values based on Christian behaviour.

Many people speak of a new spiritual age and the need for a new faith. This may sound heavy but if you consider it pragmatically there is a human need for faith. This would explain why religion has been replaced by alternative beliefs and alternative faiths. For some, green is a faith as strong as believing in God, while others seek belief in more fringe ideas.

What we could be seeing over the next decade is a re-evaluation of society and its values. The economic recession has been blamed on financial greed; profit without concern for the planet or people. When ordinary middle class people in Iceland have to be given food parcels and families in the UK are being made homeless, while building societies and banks auction off their homes for less than half their value, it is no wonder the public are questioning the state of things.

Ethics isn't just about the environment, it's also about people. In the recent recession, while the environment is losing out, people and community values are increasing. In times of trouble we band together and unite. The recession creates a sort of war-time camaraderie.

The sense of community is increasing, and data from the National Audit Bureau reveals that we want stronger communities, despite decades of decline. Obviously the web has created a whole new concept of community but there's also a desire for real communities.

THE PURITAN PURPOSE

It's what I see as the rebirth of a new form of Puritan culture – people are seeking community and starting to think again about the 'greater good'. I call this the Puritan Purpose because it's similar to the underlying values of the fore-fathers of the New World, the Puritans and similar to those of the Quakers who established many businesses based on ethics.

With a belief in community and working as a collective they sought capitalism with a moral purpose and a con-science. They looked upon business as a service to society, making money was good if it served the community but bad if it only served the individual and worse, if it damaged the community. With a strong work ethic and by being well organized they built well run companies, but values and ethics were more important than wealth. Many American companies were established on Puritan ethics, Ford being one.

In 'The Protestant Ethic and the Spirit of Capitalism' (published in 1930) Max Weber observed that the rise of middle class trade occurred chiefly among Protestants. Weber found many connections between the Protestant ethic, the spirit of modern capitalism and a spirit of indi-vidualism, with the emphasis on working hard and having a good conscience about making money. This was in con-trast to the long-standing Catholic view that poverty was inherently virtuous and only the poor are rewarded in heaven. By contrast, Samuel Willard, the last of the Puritans (1640–1707), theorized that 'riches are consistent with god-liness, and the more a man hath, the more advantage he hath to do good with it'.

PROFIT OVER PEOPLE

When you pick up the paper and see a bank, supermarket or oil company making millions per minute how do you feel? Over the last few decades large corporations have boasted publicly about their wealth, a wealth few of us benefit from. So is it any wonder that the new consumer is more willing to buy from an organization that practices 'capitalism with a moral purpose' rather than one whose only driving force is greed?

None of us like the fat greedy person who takes and never gives, Brands are no different; let's not forget that much of the purpose of branding is to make a faceless organization have human-like personality. Unfortunately for many organizations their brand is the fat, ugly, selfish money grabbing person we all hate.

Smarter organizations are waking up to this fact and are realizing that it's better to talk about the good they've done for the world and its people and not how it's given big dividends to a minority. Caring about the community shouldn't just be a CSR initiative it should be at the core of a company's ethos.

Many religious groups saw money as a reward that empowered them to do good, but our modern ethical view point of money is that most shareholders care only about the money for their own ends. Even kids see those brands that put profit first as 'bad brands', their own words. A group of 15–18 years olds we worked with on a project had enlightening views of brands. For them, greed was the main definer of badness, the second was exploitation.

If all that drives your business is meeting financial targets then it replaces any good ethos you had and inevitably you will behave in unethical ways. If you use a reduction in profits to justify sacking people, screwing suppliers or neglecting your social responsibilities, what message does that send out? BT announced in the last quarter of 2008 that it was axing thousands of jobs because its profits were down. That was a big PR disaster. You may well think that they were making a loss like Woolworth's and had to take drastic action, far from it. In fact, they were actually making an astronomical profit – their first-quarter profit was £613m. Cutting staff was all about reducing the overhead in order to increase the profits. So who ends up doing the work of those who have departed? Those left behind of course. This is the unethical situation which shareholders have created in many companies.

BA have also suffered as a brand because of how it's behaved, yet you never hear Virgin bragging about profits or saying it was laying off thousands of family bread winners in order to increase profits for a few shareholders. Virgin really understands brand reputation and the importance of its relationship with the public and the trust it's built up. It's one of the best marketed brands of all time. No other brand generates so much trust. It doesn't have to save a rainforest to be seen as ethical, it's an honest and fair brand that respects people, and that for many people makes it ethical (even if it does fly planes).

Throughout history revolutions have been a moment of rebalancing society. France and Russia saw the common people take back what a minority had taken away. Cromwell fought for social justice and to regain power from both the King and his corrupt aides. Today that minority aren't kings, warlords or the aristocracy but corporations. Where once we would have had a revolution in the form of war and fighting in the streets, this revolution is actually going on silently in the supermarket. It is as much a reaction against corporations as it is a positive act towards a better world.

THE QUAKER WAY

The triple bottom line (people, planet, profit) isn't a new concept. The early Quakers in the 18th century were opposed to a society that seems very similar to todays. Driven by materialistic values and class, they saw the purchase of fashionable styles and discarding what had been bought a month ago as shallow and wasteful (today we call it fast fashion). Quakers do not think that we should be judged on material possessions. They believe in respect, honesty and decency, taking the Christian value of treating others as you'd like to be treated yourself. Making money was only morally acceptable if the business respected people and the community. In Cadbury's early days its staff were housed, schooled and looked after by the company. A far cry from the attitude of its biggest competitor today, Nestlé.

Other Quaker companies (ironically Quaker, the maker of cereals isn't a Quaker company) that are now household names, include Barclays Bank, Bryant and May matches, Clark's shoes, Friends Provident, Huntley and Palmer's, Lloyds Bank (now Lloyds TSB), Rowntree's (now Rowntree Mackintosh, owned by Nestlé) and most surprisingly Sony (it's founder was a Japanese Quaker). There are also a number of charities: Greenpeace, Oxfam and Amnesty International.

Many modern day organizations (and charities) are still based on strong Christian values, like Traidcraft or Save the Children. Business and beliefs are still working together for a better world for all.

CHARITY AND THE RELIGION OF MONEY

A recent report, the Elderman Good Purpose study, should make enlightening reading for any marketer. Far from abandoning good causes in a recession, we not only stick by them, but gather together and become more socially aware. You only have to look at any disaster or crisis to see that human beings unite when there's a common enemy (recession in this case). Seventy-one per cent of global consumers said that they were sticking to supporting good causes, and many said they were giving more. The pound (or yen, dollar, franc or euro) in your pocket can say a great deal about what people feel and think especially when the consumer is using it to make a point.

Sixty-eight per cent of people said they'd remain loyal to a brand that supported good causes in rough times (good causes can be anything from charity to the environment). Fifty-five per cent of people will buy from a brand that supports a good cause, despite costing more. And 80% think that it's important that brands support good causes.

Consumers are sticking by the ethics but what about businesses? Alas, many see environmentalism as a nice to have rather than a need to have. Saving the planet is cut as soon as the company wants to save money. In the US many marketing directors admitted that ethics was no longer top of their list.

Even without the recession we're living in a time when community is growing in part due to the internet and in part to a feeling that society has become divided and people want to get back together (a trend spotted by recent data from the National Bureau of Statistics).

Community is a very important ethic and because brands need to engage both individuals and communities they cannot ignore it. Adding community based values is a great way to engage consumers en masse.

There is a difference between 'value' and 'values'. One is about what you get for your money and the other is why you do what you do. Big corporations that abuse people and the planet, companies that put profits first and are driven only by greed and shareholder value are out.

Consumers are looking for the ethos behind the brand, and the ethos is the reason why a company does what it does. Consumers want to know that a company isn't just driven by money, we are almost returning to the era of Quaker businesses.

The blame for the recession has been laid on those that were greedy and were only interested in money. We are entering a new more spiritual age where people are embracing new values. Just as pre-revolution France became divided by values – the rich versus the poor – so we are starting to see a similar divide in society between those whose only value is profit and those that see profit as an outcome of having people and planet values.

A quote from an old article on ethical business in America reads, 'making money by being immoral is short sighted because you'll soon be found out. Making money by being moral will mean you'll succeed long term'.

SUMMARY

We can learn a lot from past values. Puritan and Quaker business models were both successful in terms of making money as well as contributing to the community. In other countries there are strong links between religious or spiritual values and business. Islamic business models are another good example. Sadly in the West lust for money has become a religion. No company that is only focused on profit can be ethical. It has to adopt the three Ps. Any business that can make a profit while delivering with regard to people and the planet is a far better run business. Exploiting people and resources in order to make money is a barrow boy business. Even the Mafia looked after their people.

13
FAIRTRADE

THE GROWTH OF FAIRTRADE

In the UK, we drink 31 billion cups of coffee and 94 billion cups of tea every year. If all that was Fairtrade just think what a difference it would make.

Of all the ethical badges you can put on a product in the supermarket fair trade is the strongest, and stronger than any environmental label. Three out of four shoppers now recognize and support the Fairtrade symbol, making it far more recognizable than the organic mark. In our own ethical shopping survey fair trade came way above all others.

Over the last five years sales have doubled in Europe and the US with the UK the leading market. We Brits purchased over £225m worth of fair trade goods in 2007. Now the label can be found on over 3000 products from tea and coffee to wine and fruit juices, chocolate to bananas, nuts and sugar. The world market is worth over 2.3 billion Euros and expanding – up 43% on 2007 – helping to support 7.5 million producers and workers in over 60 developing countries.

Brands like Percol, Clipper, Café Direct and Fair Instant have seen healthy growth, and even the supermarkets are now jumping aboard, offering more fair trade own label products.

Prices have also come down (PricewaterhouseCooper's Sustainability survey revealed that 48% of consumers were put off by high prices) making it more accessible and competitive. One threat to the Fairtrade Foundation is the massive spend behind PG tips (Unilever) that uses the Rainforest Alliance badge. This could yet dent Fairtrade tea, as the consumer sees them as much the same. The Rainforest Alliance doesn't have the same strict regulations and measures as the Fairtrade Foundation, with some calling it a badge of convenience.

Fair trade bananas sales have rocketed by 89% to £108m, thanks mainly to supermarkets such as Sainsbury's, Waitrose and M&S. Currently, Sainsbury's sells the most (29.4%) followed by the Co-op (18%) and Tesco (14.9%).

Fair trade chocolate has also been growing at over 30% year on year, helped in part by quality brands like Devine and Green & Blacks, tempting people to indulge in more ethical choices. Cadbury's recently announced its intention to make Dairy Milk (the UK's best selling chocolate) Fairtrade by 2009.

Another growth area is cotton – demand more than doubled in just one year and global sales of Fairtrade cotton products represent more than 14 million individual items, from towels to jeans.

Of the supermarkets, it is debatable if the Co-op or Sainsbury's stocks the most number of fair trade items – the latter claims to stock 160. According to a TNS survey, the fastest growing group of fair trade customers is those aged 25–34. Fair trade's biggest marketing push is Fairtrade Fortnight, which stimulates around a 30% increase in sales during that period.

TRAIDCRAFT – THE FAIR SHARE OFFER

When we launched Feel in 2002, I met Stuart Palmer of Traidcraft, Europe's leading Fairtrade supplier (and a founder of the Fairtade Foundation). We'd only just set up our office and were still planning how we were going to get our first fee paying client when one landed in our lap. Traidcraft wanted to do a share offer and despite having never done a share offer Stuart was impressed enough with our strategy and creativity to hire us. He was a great client and together we rewrote the share offer rule book.

Instead of appealing to greed we sold it on the good you would be doing for charity, rather than as an individual investment. Using images created by artists in the Third World we created a mixed media campaign (direct mail, press, poster and web) with headlines like, 'Instead of making a killing help someone make a living' and 'Share in our future and we could make you a prophet'.

The City had predicted that they'd only make £1m but we hit £3.25m, at which point they had to cap the offer. On a budget of just £100k, that was a great ROI. Much of this came down to good strategy, good media planning and consumer insight. And a trusting client, if Stuart had meddled like so many clients do it would have failed but he didn't, one of the top five clients I've worked with.

I always emphasize that customer insight is vital to success, and we took the trouble to find out what the fair trade customer was like. With most being Christians this made the Christian press an obvious choice. We used both Traidcraft's databases and purchased lists, we then ran posters within key areas relating to postcode. We hired in a specialist financial PR agency, and backed up any PR with ads aimed at direct readers on the website.

There is no greater feeling in marketing than success, especially when it exceeds the experts' expectations. And knowing that you are helping hundreds of people to live a better life; it's reason enough to get you out of bed in the morning. I've never really had that feeling selling cars, drinks or stationery.

100 YELLOW BANANAS, HANGING ON THE TREE

A short while later Traidcraft wanted to pitch to the Guardian to be their charity of the year. Alas, we didn't know that a decision had been taken, which would exclude Traid-craft from winning, but the outcome of the campaign was still positive.

On a Monday morning staff at the Guardian in Far-ringdon (London) arrived to find dozens of bananas hanging from the trees outside their offices. Each one had a message on it. A few days later a banner appeared in the street opposite with the url www.naidraug.co.uk – over 250 staff clicked on the site within a few hours. The site emphasized how we could deliver fresh news daily if picked. We also managed to get Fairtrade goods into their canteen. We made many other unusual marketing approaches but the one that created the biggest stir was sending 20 pay slips to the directors for the sum of £7.34 – the sum a typical tea picker earns in a month. These perfect fakes caused one director to complain to the accounts department before he read the slip. He finally saw the positive side of it. Despite not winning the appointment, it helped raise Traid-craft's image both at the Guardian and within the charity sector.

It proves one important rule; if you want to make a difference you need to have bottle and trust in your agency. I doubt that Stuart was feeling comfortable about all the things we did but he knew that any compromise would in turn compromise effectiveness and that means affecting people's lives.

SUMMARY

Fairtrade is the number one ethical value that the new consumer relates to because it's about people. No matter how cold we can be most of us feel for others. It's also one of the most recognized labels. Supermarket support has been vital to its success but the introduction of lesser labels backed by big spend just confuses the consumer.

14
FOOD WASTE AND
RECYCLING

FOOD WASTE AND RECYCLING

During the Second World War the nation was rationed. Food was in short supply and nothing was wasted, even potato peelings were consumed. Back then, we didn't have plastic bags, most meat, fruit and vegetables used little packaging and we used our own bags. A stark contrast to food shopping today; the average family takes home approximately a ton of groceries per year and throws away up to 25% of what we buy in packaging and food (a great deal of which has gone past its sell by date). That's like throwing away every third bag of shopping. Although on average only 5% of the weight of our shopping basket is made up of packaging, it can account for up to 25% by volume.

There is no greater measure of a society's wealth than by what it throws away. Household recycling may have quadrupled in England in the last 10 years, but the problem is that there's too much there in the first place. And even though we all tick the box on surveys that we like to recycle, the reality is that it's only because we can and have to (Barnet fines its residents if they don't).

In English homes we're now recycling 27% of household waste compared with just 15% five years ago. East Anglia recycles the most at 34%, while Londoners recycle the least at 21% (The Office for National Statistics).

The Food Strategy Report (from the Cabinet Office) reveals that the British throw away an astounding 4.1 m tonnes of food each year, costing each household £420 on average (or 6.7 m tonnes, £600 per household according to WRAP). In a separate report WRAP says that household waste is 6.3 m tonnes a year while Defra says it is 4.7 m. It's sometimes hard to know which figures are correct, issued by the different government departments.

According to WRAP, this food waste accounts for an estimated 4.4 m apples, 1.6 m bananas, 1.3 m pots of yogurt, 660 000 eggs, 550 000 chickens, 300 000 packets of crisps, 440 000 ready meals, 1.2 m sausages, 710 000 packs of chocolate or sweets, 260 000 packs of cheese, 50 000 milkshakes and 25 000 cooking sauces. And that's ignoring what goes down the sink or the toilet!

If you're wondering how they got these figures, they audited 2138 people's bins (I love the use of the word 'audit', only the government would use accountancy words), but with over 22 m homes in the UK, that's not much to base a statistic on.

Putting food into any one of the 250 landfill sites in the UK is one of the worst things we can do because as food waste rots it produces methane, a greenhouse gas 20 times more damaging than CO_2 (each of us on average creates 94 pounds of carbon dioxide every day).

DEFRA have been running a campaign to make consumers more aware, offering tips on how to avoid the problem in the first place. It's a typical advertising solution (like many government funded campaigns) to a problem that requires a different solution. Ads that lecture consumers are rarely effective and given the competition for attention, it's hard to cut through consumer indifference.

In one town in the States they're encouraging people to recycle by offering discount points for packaging brought back to the store's recycling bins. Budgens, in my own neighbourhood of Crouch End, provide a recycling bin for customers to use as they leave the shop. Unfortunately, owing to health and safety, many items are over packaged these days in the first place.

However, one company has reversed the trend. 'Unpackaged', founded in 2006 by Catherine Conway on a market stall, is now based in The Angel, London where they have taken over the old Victorian Lloyd's Dairy (a good example of reuse). They sell everything unpackaged. The store is charming and feels like you've stepped back 50 years into post-war Britain. In 2008 they won an Observer Ethical Award.

To quote architect Michael Pawlyn from their website, who makes a good point about packaging: 'It's hard to visit a landfill site without being struck by the craziness of taking very valuable minerals and resources out of the ground, using a lot of energy, turning them into short life products and then just dumping them back into the ground. It's an absolutely monumental waste of energy and resources. As someone from the fashion industry might say, it's just so last century'.

The government is committed to reducing waste and is putting a great deal of pressure on manufacturers to reduce packaging and excessive consumption, as well as waste produced directly by the food industry (much is wasted in the processing of food).

There's also pressure on councils, consumers and the government from the EU. Targets have been set to reduce the amount of household waste (not re-used, recycled or composted) by almost half, from 22.2m tonnes in 2000 to 12.2m tonnes by 2020. In 1999 the EU ordered the UK to cut biodegradable waste in dumps to 13.7m tonnes by 2010 and to 6.3m by 2020. That's almost half the UK government's target. To date, the UK is falling short of its targets, risking a fine of up to £180 million by the EU.

When you consider that in less than two hours the UK produces enough waste to fill the Albert Hall, that every person in the UK throws away their own body weight in rubbish every seven weeks and the average UK dustbin contains enough unreleased energy to run 5000 hours of television, 3500 showers or 500 baths, you have to wonder how we managed to get into such a state.

Some blame marketing; we live in a churn society where we are encouraged by advertising to be indulgent, to buy more than we need and waste what we don't. A society where everything comes in a disposable container which should carry a warning: THERE'S NO SUCH THING AS DISPOSABLE, IT HAS TO BE DISPOSED OF SOMEWHERE.

Others simply point to basic economics; we're all better off than ever before, many of us have more than we need, so we can afford to be wasteful. It's just the inevitable behaviour of a wealthy society.

PACKAGING LESS, SELLING MORE

I interviewed a representative from Dairy Crest at the IFE (International Food & Drink Exhibition) who told me one of the biggest challenges they faced (most of it was government pressure) was to reduce packaging and landfill. Recently they've teamed up with Sainsbury's to sell milk in recyclable plastic bags in an initiative aimed at reducing packaging by 75%. If all milk was sold in this way, it would take 100 000 tonnes of plastic out of landfill annually. ASDA have introduced a recyclable cardboard milk bottle made by Greenbottle in an attempt to help their consumers reduce waste.

Waste has become an important theme in the ethical marketing mix. It's not so much a benefit, however, as a dangerous negative. Few people will be impressed by efforts to reduce packaging by 25% unless it is packaged well (M&S plans to reduce packaging by 25% and make all packaging recyclable or compostable by 2012). That's expected, and going with the flow, but if you become the victim of bad publicity it'll damage your brand. And one bad article can undo thousands of pounds worth of good marketing.

While many supermarkets take small steps forward, some are making bigger leaps. ASDA has invested £50m in regional recycling centres – something they remain very quiet about, yet it represents an impressive commitment to the environment.

What may have been a benefit several years ago is now a necessity. Carbon Neutral has also fallen into this camp. Once you could score points for it, now it's either seen as a necessity or worse, spin. Within the ethical marketing arena things are constantly changing and what worked last year may not in this. Thanks in part to the media; consumers are constantly having their values remoulded. Off-setting by planting trees, bio-fuels and home wind turbines, which were once the in thing, are now out.

THE POWER OF GESTURES AS A MARKETING TOOL

Ocado, the home delivery supermarket, have come up with a simple idea that gives consumers advance warning of use-by dates (it also solves the problem of some home delivery services selling food too close to the use-by date). They simply display the products' use-by dates online and on customer receipts. This also means that customers can reduce waste because they are more aware of the food's shelf life.

It's a good 'gesture' and makes Ocado look honest and helpful, adding value to the brand and improving customer relations. So often, brands will leap at employing expensive marketing and ad campaigns when a simple gesture would do. Gestures can be used as a powerful marketing tool as they engage emotionally. We all know that a simple smile or a 'thank you' goes a long way. I recommend that you spend half an hour brainstorming small gestures you can make to the customer. Ask yourself 'what small gesture can we make to the customer that says something positive about us or just makes the customer feel good about the brand?'

Honesty is one of the cornerstones of a good brand and is central to ethical marketing. Ask how you can make an honest gesture (especially when you screw up). Instead of claiming that you're green (when you're not) tell people you're not there yet but you're working to get there. We admire those who are honest and are driven to do better.

When I worked with NatWest I tried to convince them to put jokes on the back of the receipts you get from cash machines. It was a small gesture from the bank to make you feel good (inspired by ice lolly sticks). However, bankers are not natural marketers and really don't understand people or emotions. That idea died quickly. Sadly, good ideas are rarely bought, as it's a lot easier to sell the tried and safe but the tried and safe won't get you far. If you want your marketing to make a difference you have to do things differently, like Ocado.

FROM PLASTIC BAGS TO DESIGNER BAGS

In just three days they pulled 3 000 000 bags out of the River Thames in London, that's a lot of waste. The number of bags that go into landfill is enormous. This piece of plastic, once a useful item, now represents a retailer's ethical brand values and is more a symbol of waste than whatever goes in it. The bag has become a symbol for the green debate. Even Peter Jones (of 'Dragon's Den' and a tycoon) has jumped on the green bandwagon by backing 'The Little Bag of Bags', a bag to put all those bags in.

There's no debate that plastic bags are an indulgence and when added up contribute to landfill; however, they are one of the most reused items in our shopping. We all keep a few in the drawer for putting rubbish in, etc. Argos used to sell a device for turning old newspapers in to fire bricks, why hasn't anyone come up with a way to turn old carrier bags into something useful? I have seen them made into menu covers.

The supermarkets have ducked and dived around this issue, first introducing 'a bag for life' and finally charging for bags. One of the first to take the plunge was M&S who now charge 5p. This has resulted in an 80% reduction in bags used while Tesco has achieved a 25% reduction in carrier bags. Wholefoods are axing plastic bags all together and only provide paper bags, though when I did in store research into their customers a checkout assistant revealed that few customers want the paper bags, they prefer to put the plastic ones into the back of their 4 × 4s.

ANYA HINDMARCH: 'I'M NOT A PLASTIC BAG'

When Sainsbury's launched the designer alternative to the humble carrier bag they could not have predicted just how fashionable it would be. When it began the 'We Are What We Do' project with designer Anya Hindmarch was a little more down to earth. The aim was to make it fashionable not to use plastic bags. 'I'm Not A Plastic Bag' was designed to be a stylish, practical, reusable bag intended to raise awareness of this issue and spark debate. David Robinson, founder and chair of the global social change network called 'We Are What We Do' approached Anya with the idea. They had already published a book, 'How to Change the World for a Fiver', which proposed 50 measures that anyone could take in order to help save the planet, such as 'smile at old people because they know lots of good stuff' and 'turn off the water when you're brushing your teeth'. The first step was 'decline plastic bags whenever possible'. They wanted to take the success of the book into a project.

When the bag was launched it caused a great sensation and quickly sold out, becoming the must have fashion accessory of the year. They were even selling for hundreds of pounds on eBay. Sadly, it also sold to a lot of shallow Sloane Ranger types who had little understanding of its real meaning. Success was followed by criticism and soon eco journalists were attacking its source – China – and its carbon footprint. Questions over the use of cheap Asian labour dented its image. But it inspired a range of copy cats and helped highlight the movement away from cheap plastic bags.

THE WAR ON JUNK MAIL

The marketing industry has also come under fire (though unfairly) in some people's eyes, for junk mail, catalogues and directories. Direct mail actually accounts for just 1.5% of household waste (0.9% unaddressed, 0.6% addressed) and even those figures may be exaggerated due to questionable measuring techniques (they literally open bags of rubbish and count what's in it). By contrast, magazines and newspapers account for 11.4% and this is getting worse with the popularity of free newspapers (London has three dailies and several weeklies). The worst offender must be the Sunday papers with their masses of supplements and additional advertisements. I did a little test one weekend and cut out all the ads from one of the Sunday paper packages. The ads weighed more than the rest and more than all the pizza leaflets, door drops and junk mail I received in one week. Perhaps the government should look at Sunday magazines rather than direct mail. Though I can't

understand why the Yellow Pages and the telephone direc-
tory are needed to such an extent in this digital age and
why millions are dumped on the doorsteps of people who
don't want or need them. Most will end up in either landfill
or recycled. Add up all the printing, delivery and collection
and the Yellow Pages couldn't be less green. Ironically,
some councils have declared war on direct mail but con-
veniently ignore the vast quantity of junk they put through
the letterbox. In my area Haringey council put twice as
much junk through my door than the rest put together. This
is the great hypocrisy of ethics; reality is replaced by politics
and decisions are made based on the wrong facts. Councils
are using ethics as a marketing tool in order to make them
look good and caring; in reality, it should be defined as
propaganda.

SUMMARY

Packaging is a big issue but perhaps more for the government and councils than the consumer. This is especially so
with serious fines being imposed by the EU over landfill.
It's a sticky issue as health and safety demands impose a
level of over packaging, as do the practical needs of distribution. Reducing packaging isn't the only option, there's
the choice of selling loose or second life packaging – giving
it another use. I've seen some innovative packaging solutions – a great one for tea that uses no glues – and my
friend Kevin Perry (one of the UK's leading paper engin-
eers) has some amazing ideas. With a little bit of imagination and innovation it's amazing how you can be not only
more eco-friendly but also make your packaging a selling
feature.

15
RECYCLING FOR RESALE

TURNING LEAD INTO GOLD

It's a lot easier to throw things away but as the eco slogan used in the Shell ads goes, 'there is no away'. It's all got to go somewhere and landfill is getting filled up. Of course if we had kept to our post-war mentality of the three Rs, 'repair, reuse and recycle' (reduce and redefine are two modern additions), we wouldn't be in the mess we are in today. It's now progressively harder to repair things when many items are designed to be irreparable, it's called 'built-in obsolescence'.

I was staying recently with a friend in Spain who has a TV that is at least 10 years old. The remote had packed up and the TV didn't have any buttons to change channels. It was too old to use with one of those modern multi-functional remotes. My thought was to go and look at the new flat screens in the local electrical store. She was shocked by my attitude, 'I'll get it repaired', she said. 'No chance', I replied. 'You won't be able to get spare parts for it'. Now that's exactly how we've been taught to think in the UK. We've been sold a behaviour pattern that is part of the built-in obsolescence culture. Less than an hour later she returned with it fixed. You see, in small towns in Spain they still have a guy who fixes things, anything. People only buy a replacement when they really can't repair it. This guy knows how to fix even things that seem unfixable. In the UK we don't think that way, which is one reason why we churn so much.

But there is a changing attitude. The government, business machines, PCs, domestic appliances and white and brown goods companies are facing growing social pressure (not to mention the WEEE requirements) not to be part of the problem of waste. If the electrical goods we bought lasted 50% longer (as they used to do) think how much less landfill that would be. If they just stopped designing them to be irreparable (or stopped using screws with special heads so we can't open them) just think how many items would have a second life.

One major project that's considering its after life is the 2012 Olympics. The buildings in London will be the most eco friendly of all Olympics, with a low carbon footprint, wood from sustainable sources, low energy requirements and lots of other eco benefits that tick many green boxes. Afterwards, there are plans to ship part of the stadium to America to be recycled, with 55 000 seats being sold to a US business.

Recycling (or second life) doesn't have to be worthy or to look politically correct, it can be about fun too. And even culture! London Zoo recently attracted more visitors than usual with a series of dinosaurs made from old car tyres. Turning junk into art has become a popular theme and there are now a number of artists who have made it their signature. There are also companies turning junk such as car tyres into shoes, crash surfaces for climbing centres and even mouse mats. It's amazing how many uses old car tyres have, besides a kids' swing or as crash barriers at go-karting tracks.

Where there's lead there's gold, which is why thieves have been nicking lead off church roofs for years. Scrap metal is worth money but only scrap merchants think that way. If the public saw a value in everything they threw away they'd behave differently. With the rising price of steel, thieves have been championing recycling in a rather odd way, stealing old second hand cars and selling them to scrap merchants.

A series of TV commercials highlighting how cans can be recycled has made consumers aware but we need a more powerful and situation relevant awareness campaign if we really want consumers to change their cognitive behaviour. Who sits watching TV wondering what to do with a soda can? Why are government ads always on TV rather than in the right place? By the next day you'll have forgotten the ad. Why is there no message on public bins? Every bin should carry a marketing message to make us think. This is a simple but highly relevant piece of targeting – right place, right time, right frame of mind. How about a talking chip in your flip top kitchen bin, 'are you sure you want to throw that away, it may have another value, remember one person's rubbish is another's gold'. Or what if we had to pay to lift the lid? And shouldn't offices put all bins as far away from desks as possible in order to discourage staff from throwing paper in it instead of the recycling bins? Scottish and Southern energy have removed all the bins from their offices.

SECOND LIFE PACKAGING

Rather than use terms like 'reuse' I prefer the term 'second life packaging' or 'second life use'. If we talk in this way it takes us away from thinking of using something in another way as inferior. It also challenges packaging and product designers to think again. And who knows, if we adopt 'second life' as a normal way of thinking one day we'll be able to move to third life.

There's little doubt that our food and other household products are over packaged, we throw away at least two black bags of used packaging a week in my house. In some cases there is little room to change – health and safety regulations and security and economics dictate a great deal of packaging.

Perhaps if manufacturers aren't willing to reduce over packaging they could be encouraged to see packaging as having a second life. Companies like Gü use real glass containers and after you've had the pleasure of a chocolate cheesecake you can have the pleasure of owning a lovely glass dish. If companies were encouraged to design a second life into all packaging we'd probably see some amazing ideas.

At one agency I sent out a series of new business mailers on the back of used cornflake packets and bits of cardboard packaging we picked up in the street and from supermarket dumpsters. The campaign made a relevant point about recycling and stood out against those plush self-promotional mailers that other agencies sent out. It received an amazing response rate, exceptional for direct mail. Everyone we saw was both surprised and engaged by it, proving that it's not big budgets you need for effectiveness but good targeting, the right message and good creative thinking.

NEW BRANDS FROM OLD

A whole new business has grown out of recycling materials, and a range of new brands, my favorite is Remarkable. Each item, rulers, mouse mats, files and pads, tells you what it's made from, 'I USED TO BE A CAR TYRE'. The brand has personality and the products are of excellent quality.

Many brands use promotional gifts to support sales and marketing and now there's a full array of recycled pens made from old CDs, rulers from old water cups, etc. It's ironic that promotional marketing is driving so many eco ethical products; as main brands become eco sensitive and need to be above criticism everything that's greener is a better choice. Forget cheap pens, now they have to be made from recycled something to be CSR acceptable.

For those who think that advertising is a form of pollution (well they may well be right) a unique project designed to recycle ads is helping fight poverty by supporting local people. Trashe Bolsas is a project based in Manila which recycles large billboards into bags; I do need to point out that these ads are printed on giant tarpaulins (not paper) which are cut up and sewn into carrier bags. The designs are novel, consisting of small parts of the advertising images, with that great pixilated effect. Another amazing item is a handbag which a small charity, Bottletop, are importing. The bag is made from ring pulls and looks amazing. They are also producing a belt and other accessories.

A FANTASTIC WAY TO MARKET YOUR BRAND'S ETHICAL CREDENTIALS

Coca-Cola has found a creative way to market its waste problem, turn all your plastic bottles into clothing, complete with slogans on them such as MAKE YOUR PLASTIC FANTASTIC and REHASH YOUR TRASH. The new range of t-shirts could see up to 7000 million bottles ending up in the bottom drawer rather than landfill (though you have to make sure you don't use a hot iron on them). They have also been expanding into other areas such as bags, caps, purses and notebooks. Well, it's an innovative solution to the problem. I wonder what happens to all that stuff once you get bored with it, it probably joins the Primark junk fashions that go into landfill.

However, it's one of many projects that Coke has invested in and is starting to build its reputation as a more responsible brand. Coke, like McDonald's and Exxon, are easy targets because of their size, but as I have said previously, one small change by Coke really does make a world of difference. Perhaps we'll see a recycled version of their greatest ad of all time – a hundred people singing, bottle in hand, on a landfill site with the revised lyrics, 'I'd like to teach the world to recycle, and create planet harmony'.

ECO INNOVATION

According to the Mintel Global New Products Database, 328 new environmentally friendly products were launched in 2007 (compared to just five in 2002). Personally, I feel this could be way below the reality, as every day I discover lots of new creative ideas; for example, the Eco Button. This novel device sits by your computer. One tap and it sends the PC into low energy sleep mode – saving electricity while you are away from the desk. It's a great office addition that costs little and saves a lot.

A brand design company, JAM, made its name by taking industrial products and recycling them as new items. From damaged washing machine cylinders to Audi car parts, they have put many objects imaginatively to new uses. After seeing what JAM have done, a visit to a scrap yard really does get your imagination going.

When we set up Creative Orchestra, an incubator for young talent, we had 2200 square feet of amazing space in Islington and no furniture. Furniture, even when shopping at IKEA, is expensive. Luckily, we found a friendly agency which we knew had moved to new offices and had a load of surplus desks and so we managed to kit out much of our office for free. They had found that selling second hand office furniture is impossible and you end up paying someone to take it away to the dump. Useful sites like Freecycle are good (though crudely designed), but what we need is a more efficient network in order to recycle stuff. There have been a number of businesses, like Green Works, a not for profit organization selling second hand office furniture. Businesses throw away a lot of furniture, much ends up in landfill for lack of any buyers. Green Works not only resells office furniture, it also converts it into other pieces such as children's furniture.

If we encouraged both companies and consumers to see both alternative uses and the creative potential, we'd reduce landfill dramatically. How many offices throw away before they think? But it requires leadership. There is a schools' project that encourages kids to be imaginative but what if the government ran a campaign, or better still a big brand like IKEA? Much of their stuff is not suitable for recycling, even if it's made from sustainable sources, so why not reuse? Simple thinking like that can say a lot about a brand and by encouraging consumers to take action the brand gets the ethical glory.

SUMMARY

They say that people with low IQs also lack any ability to see the next step ahead. A stupid child who drops a brick from a railway bridge doesn't think about the consequences of his actions. Well, we in marketing aren't stupid so we have no excuse. We have to start asking, 'so what happens next?' When they've eaten the food, drunk the coffee, opened the box, what happens next? Once we ask the question we start to seek solutions and take a more responsible attitude. And when we do they become marketing benefits.

16
TURNING RECYCLING INTO GOOD MARKETING

HOW COKE SEE PLASTIC DIFFERENTLY

For a brand that may be seen as 'evil', along with McDonald's, Coca-Cola has been doing some amazing things. They have even distributed condoms and supported clean water projects in Africa, funded many good causes and launched and backed many innovative recycling initiatives.

The 'See Plastic Differently' campaign aims to show that plastic bottles are not just waste but can be reused with a bit of imagination (Blue Peter meets JAM design). Coke promoted a range of Christmas decorations and trees that were made out of recycled Coke bottles, designed by both ex-Blur member Alex James and design duo Basso & Brooke. It doesn't really tackle the problem because come January they'll join all those real Christmas trees heading for landfill, but it's fun. Personally I'd run a schools and college competition to find a long-term solution, tap into the imagination of the masses and give a massive prize to the winner – £100 000 (Coke can afford it).

Coke has also come up with fantastic plastic by turning used plastic bottles into clothing, complete with slogans on like MAKE YOUR PLASTIC FANTASTIC and REHASH YOUR TRASH. The new range of t-shirts, part of their Drink 2 Wear campaign, could see up to 7000 million bottles ending up in the bottom drawer rather than landfill. They are also extending into other areas such as bags, caps, purses and notebooks.

HOW TO ENGAGE CONSUMERS TO RECYCLE

Another marketing venture has been 'Talent From Trash', a 12-week programme targeting male football fans and harnessing their love of the game so as to encourage them to recycle more of their rubbish. The incentive is to earn money through recycling, to support their football club's youth development programmes, helping the clubs invest in future talent and success. Each time a person makes a daily pledge, they are also entered into a free prize draw. Their club can win an extra £10000 and they could personally win £5000. On average, each club earned over £4000 with Brentford FC earning over £23000. The campaign also won in the Culture, Media and Sport category in the Food and Drink Federation (FDF) Community Partnership Awards. It's a very clever marketing campaign as it combines the environment (recycling) with community and social values. And it engages people through something they have passion for. Not surprisingly, the campaign was very successful, increasing recycling levels by over 5% on average across the 13 councils that participated.

One of my favourite examples of recycling, and I use them in my creative workshops, are a series of animals made from soda cans (Fanta, Coke, Lilt). The cans are cut up into thin strips and bent and twisted to form a giraffe or a gecko. It's amazing how creative people are when they have to try and escape poverty.

FROM ADS TO BAGS

Of course Coke aren't the only ones turning recycling into cash. Trashe Bolsas is a project based in Manila that recycles ads into bags. Finally, a good use of ads many may say. I do need to point out these ads are printed on giant tarpaulins (not paper) which are cut up and sewn into carrier bags. The designs are novel with small parts of ad images on them and with that great pixilated effect. The project helps support local people and the profits are also helping to clean up a local waterfall.

Another amazing item is a handbag which the small charity Bottletop are importing. The bag, made in Salvador, Brazil, is made from hundreds of ring pulls and looks amazing. They are also producing a belt and other accessories. Bottletop also import an unusual collection of items made from bottletops (mainly from soda bottles) which include a bag, jewelry and t-shirts adorned with bottletops. The charity has established links with many top musicians, including Fat Boy Slim, bringing together fashion and music.

BEACH COMBING FOR NEW IDEAS

An inventive campaign by Saatchi & Saatchi in the US takes a different twist on recycling in order to highlight beach pollution in LA as part of a campaign for the Surfrider Campaign. Agency staff collected up all the rubbish on Venice Beach and packed it into styrofoam dishes (those uneco trays) like seafood and placed them in farmers' markets with the label CATCH OF THE DAY. Beautifully packaged cigarette butts, condoms and other trash certainly drove the point home. Added to this, they also built sand sculptures of sea animals, highlighting that the sand sculptures were disappearing as fast as the real thing. When they collapsed a buried sign was revealed with the headline 'Pollution and beach development are destroying marine life. This quickly'.

THE REAL ART OF PERSUASION

One of my favourite and most innovative environmental projects is one by a Brighton based artist, Ptolemy Elrington.

Elrington drags old shopping trolleys from rivers and canals, cuts them up and remakes them into amazing wire sculptures of creatures. A heron, osprey, kingfishers, frog, water vole and a dragonfly are just a few examples.

Having seen his art, Elrington was commissioned by Anglian Water to create wire sculptures to highlight the rubbish thrown into rivers as part of the RiverCare campaign (designed to keep rivers clean). The funding came from the Arts & Business New Partnership and was supported by the Environmental Agency. The sculptures were placed on the river edges to make people more aware. As a piece of ambient marketing it was highly effective as it's both different and emotionally engaging, and good for PR. Never underestimate art's power to persuade. It's bang on the ethical button as it highlights pollution in an innovative way that you'd remember for far longer than any ad. Too often we resort to the old techniques of ads and direct mail when thinking outside the media box is both more effective and less expensive.

Elrington also runs a project called 'hubcap creatures' and has made the most amazing creatures mainly from old car hubcaps. His sculptures range from fish to a giant dragon. Check it out on the web, amazing stuff.

SUMMARY

One man's waste is another's treasure. Even better when that treasure feeds and supports small communities in the developing world. Big brands that embrace ethical values can make big changes in the world, not just because of their scale but because of their influence. Engaging the consumer and working together isn't just common sense but good marketing. And sometimes the outcome may not be the traditional ad solution but a metal kingfisher made out of a shopping trolley.

17
THE ETHICAL SPHERE

THE ETHICAL SPHERE

Back in 2006 at BLAC, myself, Matthew North (a planner) and Gary Shannon (account director) started to pen out what initially became the Ethical Wheel. We were pitching for Scottish & Southern Energy's green product. It has since gone through various refinements and advances to end up as the Ethical Sphere.

The Sphere allows any brand to identify its correct ethical values and how appropriate they are for marketing purposes. So often brands jump on the green bandwagon and waste a fortune on the wrong ethical message, missing the one that could make a difference to sales or brand image. I've seen a few examples in the financial market where marketing directors think by just using the word green that's enough, it isn't.

KEY ETHICAL VALUES (KEVs)

Initially we identified over 50 ethical values covering a wide range of people and planet issues (see diagram). Many areas, such as the environmental, cover a whole range of issues from pollution to CO_2, waste, chemicals and much more. Some areas have their own specialist ethical values such as diamonds, where they've been linked to drugs and gun running (as highlighted in the film 'Blood Diamond')

Figure 17.1 The Ethical Sphere

as well as abusing workers. It's not a case of just ticking boxes on a list.

Once a wide selection has been identified, and it's always surprising how many you discover, they need to be thinned down. The final few – we called them Key Ethical Values (KEVs) – need more rigorous selection via research or market testing. It may be seen as a laborious process but as with any marketing, if the messaging is wrong, no amount of budget will sell the product. And in this market, getting the message wrong can also have a fatal backlash.

Balancing KEVs and traditional sales propositions

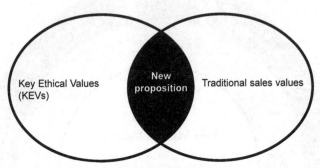

Figure 17.2 Key Ethical Values

BALANCING PROPOSITIONS

The secret of getting your ethical marketing proposition right is to know that few products sell on ethical values alone. No one wanted to buy ugly vegetables just because they were organic, they had to make them look and taste good. Fair trade fashion has to be fashionable; no one wants to wear a hemp sackcloth. People are still looking for the right thing, ethics is an added value.

THE THIRD DIMENSION

The wheel was good for a single answer but if you looked at the customer journey or even the change in the consumer behaviour of a customer, from morning to night, it was just too two dimensional. Mick Rigby, a founder of one of the more innovative media planning companies, Monkey, puts a lot of emphasis on understanding the changing mind and mood of consumers throughout the day and in different environments. This is something that is overlooked by many of the bigger media agencies I've worked with. He looks beyond the numbers and into the mindset. For example:

for a slimming product, rather than get lost in women's magazines, they asked 'when is a woman most sensitive to her weight?' The answer was when she's trying on clothes, so they ran ads on the mirrors in changing rooms – very smart.

The sphere adds the extra dimension of the customer's journey, meaning that at any touch point you can get the balance right. It sounds complicated but is actually very simple.

THE PROCESS

1. Identify broad ethical values.
2. Define KEVs (Key Ethical Values).
3. Refine and define a single ethical value.
4. Define traditional selling values (both 3 & 4 requires understanding consumer trends and insights).
5. Combine propositions.
6. Define customer journey and channels/database (remember – right place, right time, right frame of mind).
7. Convey your message in as creative and engaging way as possible (remember most ads are ignored, don't let yours be one of them).

SEEING THINGS DIFFERENTLY

I can guarantee that almost anyone using the Ethical Sphere will be surprised to find themselves in a very different place from where they started. As mentioned elsewhere, we used this process in order to move cleaning products from environmentally friendly to friendly to the home environment. In applying the 50 plus ethical values we discovered a few we hadn't considered. Just using broad terms like 'environmentally friendly' is a bit too vague, you need to dig and define. The product was free from chemicals, had natural ingredients, the packaging was all recyclable (even down to the spring in the spray head) and the, being new, factory had fantastic ethical credentials (low energy use, water recycling, etc). The staff were given days off in order to support community projects and the firm supported several charities. The more we dug the more ethical values we were able to tick off. Ok, it fell down on transport and not being local but nothing ticks all the boxes.

We then looked at all those values in the context of consumer values and benefits and against different consumer groups – mums and babies, singles, empty nesters, family and teen kids, couples (no kids), different income levels, different buying habits, etc. There are many variants to consider.

The final focus was on mums and kids and on being chemical free. Thankfully, the product was first rate at cleaning but when you become a mother your number one priority is your child, not the rainforest. So as nice as an environmental cleaner is, it's not top of the list. However, when a mother discovers that the reason it's kinder to the environment is because it contains no nasty chemicals and only safe natural ones, that means it's also kind to you and your family. Compare that to the chemical alternatives such as Mr Muscle or Cillit Bang. Suddenly the ethical values have more relevant propositions and benefits to mum.

BROADER THINKING

In another case we applied the Ethical Sphere to an electric car and arrived at a very different proposition. Again they were using broad based ethical umbrella terms that really mean little and are so overused they have little impact. By contrast we identified 12 KEVs, and three very powerful ones.

The Ethical Sphere isn't a magic wand or the ultimate tool but it works for one reason – it challenges us to think more broadly, with open minds and to apply a valuation process to our decision making. If you want a shortcut, just think with an open mind and from the consumer's viewpoint. Avoid broad based terms and green clichés and remember, no matter how worthy your product is, you still need to sell it. As the old saying goes, 'it doesn't matter if you build a better mousetrap, if you don't market it no one will buy it'.

SUMMARY

Ethical marketing isn't just about bolting on a few eco words such as 'green'. I see so many campaigns that are a waste of a company's hard earned money. Like any good marketing you need to develop the correct strategy and proposition. Understanding consumer insight is essential. You need to find the right pitch, so build in a test. With so many angles, you need to do your thinking up front – you can't rush it – or your marketing spend will be as good as putting it in landfill.

18
LANGUAGE AND PERSUASION

THE POWER AND INFLUENCE OF WORDS

In marketing, words have power. The right word or the wrong word can make or break a campaign. In the ethical arena some words have become devalued while others are highly influential, and many are confusing. The context in which words are used is also important. The word 'green' on packaging is more credible than seeing it on an ad – in fact ads using the word 'green' are less likely to be believed than those without it.

Words are like brands, they come with values, meanings and associations. They can be a shortcut to triggering ideas and associations in a consumer's mind. Some words have changed meaning over the decades; others have taken on new values. However, if you ask people to write down associations with a single word, each of us will put down something different. I do this exercise in workshops with words such as 'love', 'creativity' and 'green'. We ask people to write down seven words and then compare one list to six others. Amazingly very few words are repeated between the lists, maybe one or two at most. Try it. By nature we all have our own folio of associations, so if I use a word like 'green' in a headline it can give out different messages to different people. Deep greens latch onto it optimistically; cynics may be defensive and see greenwash.

SUSTAINABILITY

I was listening to a piece on the radio about 'should the banking industry be more moral in these worsening times?' I think the piece was targeting its profit over people and planet approach; let's be honest the City may well spend loads of money on philanthropic projects, and its support of many charities is great but then it can afford it. However, its reputation as a moral crusader is somewhat limited. During the piece a woman from the banking world was interviewed and used the 'sustainability' word, but obviously totally missed the point of the programme: 'We need to make sure the banking industry is more sustainable and can continue to make a healthy profit'. When all you can think and care about is money, even eco-ethical words like 'sustainability' can be adapted to your own values.

Conscientious consumers are facing a few dilemmas over cotton, a market that is exploding and is now worth over £1bn. What is the difference between 'organic' and 'sustainable'? To many consumers it sounds the same but using the term 'sustainable' has been banned in ads in the UK because it's misleading and has been dubbed a greenwash term. Most organic cotton comes from Turkey, China and India, but a few critics suspect that there's more organic cotton sold than produced. Major brands, like Nike, Wal-Mart, Woolworths, M&S and H&M, are all users of real organic cotton. But a trick used by some retailers is related to content. Mixing in a small quantity of organic cotton (as little as 5%) has allowed some retailers to suggest that items are organic. The general public can be easily fooled though smarter greens will see through any such claims. It does demonstrate the belief held by retailers that ethics is a selling point, but it also shows the low moral depths some big brands sink to in order to flog things.

By comparison with the UK, 'sustainability' is more commonly used in the US. In the UK, along with 'carbon', it leaves many consumers blank. The problem with communication often lies in the words we use. Many of the words used (especially in the environmental arena) come from scientists and experts who use technical jargon. We need a whole new consumer friendly language. 'No GM' means what to a consumer? If they recall reading articles about genetically modified food several years ago when it was well covered in the press then maybe GM has some depth of meaning. Instead, it just becomes a badge of badness.

Marketing eco-ethical values needs to start with the benefits to the consumer, even if those benefits are indirect – i.e. saving the planet. The phrase 'doing my bit' is a good example of turning an outcome into a consumer benefit.

CARBON FOOTPRINT

'Carbon footprint' and 'tyre footprint' are examples of terrible naming. Firstly, 'carbon' is a confusing term. What do you think of? That black stuff on a barbecue or in the fireplace or a pencil? Then there's the term 'footprint'. If the powers that be exercised a little thought they would never use this term, instead they'd spend a little time branding it with a term consumers can understand. It's a complicated idea and most people don't like complicated ideas.

The number one rule is to keep it simple. But most of the time the terms come out of scientific space and into the media. In one survey that we conducted, the narrative feedback we received from asking people about carbon footprints highlighted how the consumer had no idea what it really meant. They can't relate to it. 'Is that the black powder they put into urns after you're cremated?' And an ad that uses a pun by showing people leaving black footprints everywhere is only adding to the confusion. Personally, I think people tag along with the idea rather than understand it, 'I guess if it's got a lower carbon footprint it must be better' is about the level of understanding. But wouldn't it be so much better if we really got it? VW did manage to come closer than the Act on CO2 campaign with their balloon ad for their Blu Motion Polo where large balloons were used to visualize how much CO2 is released from cars and appliances.

POLLUTION HAS POWER

Cars have always had the image of being bad for the environment but that powerful word 'pollution' has been abandoned in recent years in order to concentrate on the 'carbon' language – a big mistake in my opinion. 'CO2' is very scientific language which is never a good way to appeal to the general public. 'Act on CO2' means what to the punter in the street? It's a nice marketing package for government departments, it makes them look like they are acting on something, but as is true with most government campaigns, it's more about the politics of looking good than the greater good. Of course if you spend millions you get a result like the hooked campaign for stopping smoking, but figures released at the time to defend the campaign from critics suggested that the cost to the tax payer of the average smoker giving up was £7000 per head.

Consider the phrase 'Act on pollution for a cleaner world' – it sounds more important and is more emotive. Add in a reference to our kids and who wouldn't take action? The word 'pollution' is loaded with generations of understanding that car exhaust is bad, from the lead debate of the 70s that forced the introduction of lead free fuels to images of smog-bound cities in Asia. Words are like brands, they come with a history and are a shortcut in people's minds to a collection of values. It'll take a generation at least to get 'CO2' anywhere near to the negative level that the word 'pollution' has achieved. However, the problem is that the wrong people are steering the debate.

CO2

It's frightening how few people even know what H_2O is. But then you also have to consider that the vast majority of kids have no idea that ham comes from a pig. There is an easy confusion between CO_2 and CO, carbon monoxide, the stuff that kills families in holiday villas when the heating is faulty. One is ok to breathe and the other will kill you. But if you recall your biology lessons we release CO_2 which is good for trees because they breathe CO_2 and release oxygen, so most people's first impression in their mind of CO_2 is a good one. Undoing that isn't easy.

The government's Act on CO_2 campaign is a very nice advertising campaign, from a well put together website, to great posters and a novel TV ad with cute little engines driving around. The ads are largely fact based – make sure your tyres are properly inflated, don't over rev engines, etc. Great stuff but as a campaign that's likely to make people act it has a weak call to action. It's about as influential as telling a smoker that smoking kills.

A friend of mine worked in Africa on a project educating people about AIDS. Despite many advertising campaigns the message was being ignored, even by people who had lost members of their family to AIDS: 'In Africa you can't talk *at* people you need to talk *to* people. You need to engage them, you can't tell them, they don't want a lecture, you need to help them understand'. It was Confucius who said, 'Tell me and I forget. Show me and I remember. Involve me and I understand'.

Their solution was to involve people in a theatrical workshop. People were able to understand better through interaction and engagement. My own experience with dealing with the youth market and Family Planning campaigns for the use of condoms is that kids ignore traditional advertising messages, especially those that look like they are coming from somewhere that represents authority.

In the West we forget that we aren't any different from our cousins in Africa. To communicate effectively you need to engage people, not talk at them. Since I've installed an Owl, an electronic device that shows my electricity usage, I've started taking action. I look at the device and it makes me think. It has made me realize just how much electricity normal household lights use if left on. If cars came with a CO2 measuring device on the dashboard we'd think twice about driving our kids to school when they could walk (and get healthier in the process).

GREEN

'Green' is one word that has a powerful meaning. Most people get it, though it's started to lose its focus, and people are using it to cover a broader field than just environmental issues. Organic cotton may be green yet I wouldn't call Fairtrade cotton green but ethical. Many people issues are referred to as green. Its definition within society has become blurred but it has retained its positive meaning. Green means good (unless it's in an ad).

One online research project in the US gave ads a 17% rating for believability but ads making environmental claims just 14%. That's a 3% reason not to use the word 'green' in ads.

What is interesting about the word 'green' is that it's a visual word, and people are mainly visual (see the section covering NLP). 'Sustainability' and 'CO2' are very analytical words because they have come out of the scientific community who think rationally and analytically – just how the general public don't think. The word 'pollution' has become a visual word. It instantly triggers a cloud of grey in your mind. If you put it on a tin of paint you'd expect it to be grey.

There are many other words floating about – more than a few eco-bolt ons – and many more that will come on to the scene. But in the area of marketing how you use words depends on three things: the audience's understanding of that word, the context it's placed in (packaging, ads, websites) and the quality of writing (good copy sells, bad doesn't). It's important not to assume that everyone understands the meaning you think words have and worse, to think that just using words like 'green', makes you green. In fact, avoiding clichéd eco-ethical words may be a better way to convey your message.

SUMMARY

We often take words for granted, never stopping to question or think about what they really mean and how they mean different things to different people. There's an exercise I do in my workshops that really opens people's eyes to how everyone sees words differently. Too many brands think that it's all about the words. So they take the fads of the moment, bolt them onto corporate messages and throw them about like candy. Words have power, for both good and bad. Beware how you use them.

19
HOW TO BE A CREATIVE MARKETER

WHY BE CREATIVE?

'Minds are like parachutes, they perform better when open'. This is a quote I open many of my lectures with, the other is 'If you follow conventional thinking, all you'll ever be is conventional'. Throughout this book I'm asking people to be open minded, to challenge conventional thinking and be brave. 'No one buys from a dull salesman' said the legendary ad man David Ogilvy.

It's easy to follow rules but there really aren't any yet, just learning and observation. And even if there are rules, in a changing world they don't last long.

Entering the world of eco-ethical marketing requires being open to being challenged. To explore and experiment. To make mistakes because that's the only true pathway to learning.

HISTORY TEACHES US HOW TO REALLY FLY

When the Wright Brother first set out to fly they read everything they could about flight. There were self-proclaimed experts on flying and many books on the rules and science of flight. The thing was; no one had actually flown yet. After reading and trying out all these ideas they finally realized that they needed to go back to scratch. Conventional wisdom sometimes is not as wise as we think. So often we assume that experts actually know what they are talking about or that their viewpoint is the right one. We forget that what works today, especially in marketing, may not work tomorrow. This is especially true with regards to the web. You need to have a culture of 'challenge and change' at all times. Tom Peters, the business guru, recommends that all companies employ a professional maverick in order to keep the company smart.

The Wright brothers finally started with an open mind and a clean slate: 'Science theory held us up for years. When we threw out all science, started from experiment and experience, then we invented the airplane'. Inventing the airplane is not an exaggerated claim, they developed wind tunnels and much of the modern airplane is based on their findings. On 17 December 1903 (just 106 years ago) they made the first powered flight in the Kitty Hawk. Less than 40 years later the jet plane flew. Sixty-three years later man walked on the Moon.

If the first plane, with its twin wings, made of wood with a fabric skin, had become the rule for all planes where would we be today? Instead it became a starting point. Creative people adapted it, experimented and the plane changed. Thanks to a combination of technology, science, imagination and innovation we have managed to reach the stars. And who knows where next.

In the world of ethical marketing there are those that want to write a rule book. I think you'll find that this book is no rule book and adopts another quote attributed to the Wright brothers, 'there are no rules, just learnings. The rest is instinct'.

WELCOME TO FUZZY MARKETING

Alas, we live in a numerical age. You can blame the Greeks, according to my Latin teacher at school. Everything has to be measured, evaluated and quantified. We are constantly looking for the holy grail of magic numbers. By contrast, I believe that instinct is far more powerful, and I am a great champion of Fuzzy Thinking; it's what transformed Silicon Valley. Fuzzy thinks outside logic, it's a higher order of thinking and more dimensional. Dyslexics do it naturally – Einstein, the Wright Brothers, Leonardo da Vinci, Picasso, Branson and many great inventors, innovators and creatives. Entrepreneurs think fuzzy, accountants linear. Few great leaps forward were ever made through pure logic or by linear thinkers. Creative minds make the world move on; analytical minds just make it turn. As Einstein put it, 'Logic will get you from A to B but its imagination that takes you beyond'.

Several years ago I did a series of lectures and articles on Fuzzy Marketing, it was an attempt to get marketing directors to think around problems and be less reliant on numbers. Creativity isn't just about being artistic; it's just as much about new ways to solve a problem. In the world of eco-ethical marketing you need to solve many problems, only fools follow a formula. This requires looking at things in a new way.

For many years I've been doing creative workshops for many well-known blue chip brands. It always starts the same, people saying that they aren't creative. Wrong, they've just been led to believe that they aren't creative because they have been taught to follow a linear way of doing things and linear thinkers believe in process and rules (which is why they have never invented anything or furthered mankind). Once you allow people to think freely and for themselves a world of possibilities opens up. Within an hour they are amazed at just how creative they can be. The only problem is that the environment most of them work in doesn't allow for creativity. Tom Peters, the great management guru, recommends that every company hires a maverick. I agree, you need people to challenge, to be creative, to push the boundaries.

Fuzzy Logic has been around since Victorian times but was popularized by R.H. Wilkinson in the 1960s (based on the work of the mathematician Lofti Zadeh). We assume that everyone is linear in their thinking process, but we are wrong, it is the way a lot of people outside the West think. That's why someone from another culture often surprises us with the ability to think differently. One of the most successful creatives in the London advertising scene of recent years was Juan Cabral, who's from South America. He created the Sony 'Balls' campaign, the plasticine rabbits and also the humorous Gorilla ad for Cadbury's at Fallon's.

When I started the original Feel I hired a Spanish creative director, Victoria Gallardo, because she thinks differently. She's been one of my best creative acquisitions to date and is now Creative Director of the creative shop, Creative Orchestra. Latins use their feelings more and are more visual as a nation. Often overlooked by the Brits, they have a strong creative culture and their architecture is some of the best in the world. They are equally passionate about quality, so don't accept the corner cutting attitude of many clients.

The Brits, by contrast, are very logical and wordy, that's not to say we don't do great work, we do. Thankfully, the internet means we can not only see great ideas from around the world but we can also be the judge. As a consequence, I think awards will soon fade, after all they are just another measuring technique. Six people decide what's great? Like we can't make up our own minds.

HOW TO RUN A TRAIN LESS EFFICIENTLY BUT LOOK MORE EFFICIENT

Alas, as a nation we are not fuzzy thinkers and we prefer to put our trust in numbers not people or instinct. The trouble with trying to reduce the world to a binary code or a matrix, measures and targets, is that it's very two dimensional. It also leaves the door wide open to more imaginative brands. I recall a great example of the folly of numbers which I heard at a conference. Train companies are focused on arriving on time. Now there's two ways to achieve this, either run a better, more efficient service, or play with the numbers.

One company simply added 10% to its journey times, now most trains arrived on time. Another took out trains so others could travel with fewer obstructions. Both delivered a better service but the customer suffered. There was no measure for how the customer felt. Numbers are dangerous things. And targets are especially dangerous because people do crazy and sometime irresponsible things in order to meet them. Just look where big bonuses in the City has got us. The trouble is, in an unexplored area, we want to makes things as predictable as possible. We need to manage the uncertainty. Here's the shocker. Don't. Follow Edison, let the unpredictable happen and use it to learn by. Even if it fails you'll have learned something. More often than not, making big leaps achieves more than small steps.

I attended a lecture at an angel investors evening several years ago, with a speaker from the London School of Economics, who'd studied the habits of investors and risk. Angels are higher risk players than financial institutions and follow instinct as much as logic. They get a feeling that a company will succeed, due in part to the passion and drive of the individuals starting it up. Out of every five businesses they invest in, two will lose them money, two will break even, but one will rocket and pay back big time. But no one knows which one. Angel investors spread bets. All the science, guidelines and models can't predict the outcome because there is so much uncertainty. Many successful businesses don't follow the business plan because they face unpredictable factors that make them zig zag. Using this model, financial institutions should invest in five different new products and statistically one will rocket. You need to take risks and build in failure as part of the learning process. No risk, no payback. I would recommend looking at five different ethical (not just green) propositions.

BE BRAVE – GIVE YOUR STAFF A GET OUT OF JAIL CARD

A useful trick which I advise companies to adopt is the 'Get out of Jail' card. It empowers people to push the boundaries and take more risks. You give each employee a card that forms a contract; providing they're doing things for the right reasons and not being irresponsible (like being drunk) then they have permission to fail once and play the card. No criticism, no firing or condemnation. It'll be put down to an acceptable failure on the pathway to success. A simple device like this can transform a culture overnight. It forces management to accept failure as part of progress and the staff to be more progressive.

PROCESS AND IDEAS

One of the problems with having a good idea is how to get everyone behind it. This is easy when there's a crisis and companies are forced to act but when you are ahead of the game, it's an uphill struggle. An idea is only as good as the process and the process needs to be structured around getting the best talent and work out there. The problem is (and I don't blame marketing directors) that the UK (and we are not unique) loves plutocracy, red tape and process. We don't allow individuals to sign off, empowerment is rarely given and most people need to have several other signatures. That's not because these people are trying to improve the idea but because most corporations fear a mistake. This only encourages people to make comments and changes.

I've found that marketing isn't just about good ideas (it's certainly not about bad ones) but corporate structure. When one person makes the decision and takes responsibility, you get great work. When I worked with Ford our ads went through six layers. Each layer took a layer of creativity out. By the end the ad would be functional and informative but not at all engaging. Since then Ford has changed and their work is excellent – I especially like the ad featuring recycled car parts as music instruments – brilliant.

It's said that IBM has 26 layers to go through whereas the Mafia only has three. It'll probably take an age for someone from IBM to write to me to challenge this. The Mafia, by contrast, will probably send someone around within the week. But you have to agree, they know how to run a business and change quickly to market conditions (usually a load of cops in a police car). Telewest (now part of Virgin Media) was a bit like IBM. One piece had 14 different clients to sign it off. Weeks later the piece returned: 'It's a very rounded piece', the account manager commented. 'They've taken all the corners off'.

The trouble is when you push a client to tell a more ethical story it involves risk. If lots of people are signing off then someone will start with 'ummm …' and all the maybes, possibilities and myths will come out. Fear is a dangerous thing, opportunity requires balls. Most brands would rather say nothing than risk a backlash; well, except Shell and BP who have just received an award from Greenpeace for greenwash.

Back in 2004 we worked with More Than insurance, a division of Royal & Sun Alliance. The company (originally set up as RSA) were seen as a very boring and traditional brand and the insurance market was becoming full of interesting and quirky ones such as Elephant. With its strong clean green graphics and its mascot, Lucky the dog (now dead), More Than stood out in the market place. They were a great client, lovely people to work with, but the shortcoming was that the business was set up in silos. Each marketing team was working separately. The trouble with organizations that work in silos is that it's hard to find people to champion an idea if it doesn't fit within their remit. For us it seemed a great opportunity to promote green insurance, a new concept back then. But selling it in was impossible. Green insurance wasn't to happen for another two years.

My advice to any marketing director is ask yourself, is my department set up to push the boundaries and deliver the right message? Are the people involved forward thinkers or too safe? Are they able to back up the brief to the agency? Are the right people empowered and the wrong people kept out of it? There's a lot of greenwash out there because the brief was wrong. Structure and process should always be the servant of great marketing, not the other way round.

SUMMARY

It's one thing to get your strategy, messaging and media right but you need to be imaginative, innovative and crea- tive. It's a very competitive world and the vast majority of marketing is ignored. If you want to be part of that small percentage that isn't ignored you need to be brave. Market- ing budget carries with it a responsibility, if spent well it grows the business which means you help more people and do more good.

20
FAT AND FIT – OBESITY AND HEALTH

LET THEM EAT FRUIT

Marie Antoinette's famous quote 'Let them eat cake' (actually she didn't say that, it's a popular misquote) would have started a different revolution today. Given our high levels of obesity, anyone encouraging us to eat high calorie food would be hung in the press. Yet, in the UK, across Europe and in the US, billions of dollars are being spent on marketing food of every kind, most of which is still unhealthy. In the US obesity leads to 300000 premature deaths every year. Europe doesn't fare much better and Norway has a real problem with cholesterol owing to its dairy diet.

With two thirds of kids eating at home at least once a day and at least five times a week, it's at home where good eating habits start. US researchers found the best thing parents can do to help their overweight children is to cook them frequent family meals and promote physical activity in order to build up their kids' self-esteem. The emotions of a child can play havoc with their eating habits. Parents who feed their kids junk food will only be encouraging them not to value good food. You can blame the brands but it's the parents who put it in the shopping trolley and pay the bill. Educating consumers (especially parents) and changing buying behaviour are key factors in trying to reduce our obesity rates. Campaigns like 'five a day' have influenced us, with consumption of fresh fruit and veg rising steadily over the past decade, increasing to almost £8 billion of annual sales in the UK.

In Barack Obama's 'Plan for a Healthy America' he says 'Healthy environments include sidewalks, biking paths and walking trails; local grocery stores with fruits and vegetables; restricted advertising for tobacco and alcohol to children; and wellness and education campaigns'. It'll be interesting to see if during his period in office he does manage to make a significant change to the health of the US nation.

'Run for the border', a survey by Mintel, suggests that adolescents' food perceptions and actual eating habits are better than previously thought and that teens are becoming more receptive to healthy eating messages, though McDonald's is still the number one choice of fast food restaurants for the youth. There does seem to be a healthier attitude towards food developing with two thirds of teens believing that good eating gives you energy and vitality and that a balanced diet is important. Two out of five said they liked the trend towards healthier fast food. Forty-two per cent of young people go for food that gives them more energy, while 35% eat vitamin and nutrient rich foods. Only one quarter try to eat foods low in fat with 22% looking for low sugar options

One UK government report claims the majority of Brits will be obese by 2050 and only 10% of men and 15% of women will have a healthy weight within a generation. But there is good news; the Centers for Disease Control and Prevention (UK) reported in May 2008 that 'kids' and teens' obesity levels seem to be levelling off, having shown no significant increases from 1999 to 2006'. The recession has already resulted in a reduction in sales of ready meals, with families cooking at home, rather than eating processed foods. For brands, there's a move away from processed food and additives, towards more natural, healthy ingredients, with taste remaining a top priority. Convenience and value are still key factors for time poor consumers who are no longer cash rich. Those that can blend all these factors will be the winners over the next decade.

When I worked with a group of kids from Brook (the youth charity) on a rebranding project we took the opportunity to question them on ethics, food and brands. Most agreed that healthier eating was a good idea but also admitted to eating badly and at fast food places. Convenience was the main reason, followed by cost, for not eating healthily: 'When you're out you have little choice of health options. Most of the time if you only got a little cash it'd be crisps or a chocolate bar'. Taste was another issue: 'Some of the healthy options, like low cal chocolate bars or those pasta snacks taste crap'.

HEALTHY MARKETING

There has been a popular growth in healthier foods, especially those that promote disease preventative properties, beyond the nutritional content of the food. More conscientious consumers want things (they perceive to be) less processed, preferring to buy more natural products. Many shoppers are sceptical about health claim benefits but digestive health has been a new sector that has exploded, backed by big marketing budgets. Actimel and Activia now account for 57% of sales in this sector.

Another area of massive growth is in healthy eating labels, which is dominated by the supermarket own brands and is now worth almost £1.7 billion (TNS data). Tesco, Asda and Sainsbury's between them have an 80% share of own label healthy eating ranges; almost 60% is Tesco's alone. The top ranges are Tesco's 'Healthy Living' and 'Healthy Eating', Sainsbury's 'Be Good To Yourself' and ASDA's 'Good For You' brands. The supermarkets have created strong sub brands that leave little room for others to enter. This seems to be a strategy by the big brands to own categories rather than share them with independent producers. They are doing the same with ethical cleaning products.

A big increase in hypochondria and (a misbelief) in allergies and food intolerances have seen a 20% growth of free-from ranges – 25% of consumers now buy a free-from product, a category worth £190 million. Soya sales are growing 8.7% year on year with market leader Alpro having expanded the category beyond milk and into dairy. Ten per cent of households now buy a Soya product, and Soya has also found new audiences, through both taste and its association with a generally healthier lifestyle.

Brands like Alpro have a strong ethical ethos; born in 1980 they originated from a desire to tackle the nutrition problems of the Third World. They have grown through providing a quality product with an honest ethos, free from additives and marketing spin.

As part of their commitment to sustainable development, they don't buy commodity beans (many come from areas of the rainforest that have been chopped down), instead they only buy organic Soya beans from sustainable sources grown in Brazil. In April 2007 Alpro announced that they were committed to becoming a carbon neutral manufacturer by 2020, by May 2008 CO_2 emissions had already come down 24%.

Alpro has expanded the Soya market by moving into other dairy categories and has reframed itself successfully from a niche product to a mainstream healthy lifestyle brand. It's a good example of a brand that has managed to grow without compromising its ethical values.

THE GROWTH OF HEALTHY SNACKS

One area that has been growing off the back of a move towards a healthier option are snacks. It's predicted that by the end of the decade there will be a 26% increase in sales of fruit snacks, rising to £239 million and a 44% rise in sales of seeds to £39 million.

There's also been a rise in premium indulgent snack sales, as people enjoy them as a treat rather than an everyday snack. Kettle crisps, for example, have seen sales rise by 26%. Maybe that's why Walkers are trying to look so ethical all of a sudden with their locally sourced potatoes and low carbon footprint.

The recession may well hit some aspects of this market with people cutting out unnecessary purchases or shops reducing stock. Health issues have certainly hit some less healthy snack products with parents becoming more concerned about the quantity of fats and sugars they are giving their kids.

REBRANDING FAT – TAFS

When my kids were 12 and 13 we took them to Orlando and Disneyland and all the other attractions. We were amazed by how many extremely fat people we saw. I don't mean in number (we have lots of fat people in the UK) but the actual size of them. As kids are prone to say very loudly 'she's fat' we had to use the term 'tafs' (fat backwards) to refer to people. I can still recall the image of a woman so large she had to drive around on one of those small electric vehicles. Worse, as she drove past she had an enormous piece of cake in her hand.

Wherever we went we were being tempted by high fat, high calorie food and drinks. Regular Coke, burgers, sweets and more were the norm and restaurant portions were 50% bigger than in the UK. The issue was clearly cultural. Forget fast food, simply too much food was the problem that was adding inches to waistlines.

A friend recently got a job in the US at a promotional agency. In the UK she was considered overweight but post-move she found she was thin by comparison to others: 'It's great, here no-one sees me as overweight'.

The UK has become obsessed with weight, and we have one of the widest ranges of low fat, low sugars products in the world. There are few aisles in a supermarket where you can't buy a 'lite' version of a regular product. Diet Coke has become as much a recognized brand name as its 'full fat' sister Coke.

The Brits have taken to running, joining gyms and even walking up stairs instead of taking lifts. Well, some Brits. Up to 40% are not health or waistline conscious; reflected in what they buy and feed their kids (MORI published a very interesting report on who controls kids' eating). Obesity is a social issue and can't just be blamed on the marketing of high calorie junk foods. Most people have the option, in a free society they can choose. Unfortunately, many parents still choose to feed their kids crisps, fat Coke and pizza.

Where marketing can be blamed is when it spins health claims. Reducing fat but increasing sugar doesn't make a product less calorific. Yet that's exactly what some brands have done. Using the term 'lite' implies to the consumer a dramatic reduction in calories, while in fact it may only be as little as 5%. Consumers trust brands and, as mentioned in other chapters, over two thirds believe and trust packaging (most think it has to be legally correct) unlike ads. A claim that implies it's healthier, when really it isn't, is just misleading and unethical. So too is increasing the pack size, so people buy more, as crisp and chocolate companies have done. 'The Big One' may shift more of the product but in time the consumer will snap back. One crisp company was blamed for contributing towards obesity in children through heavy advertising and the use of a celebrity. Not by the press but by a House of Commons select committee. How damning is that?

A MOTHER'S DILEMMA

As mentioned earlier, despite the various claims of a generation of fat kids, teen obesity levels appear to be reaching a plateau. But obesity across all ages remains a valid concern for governments and health officials and of course educated parents. What we put into our kids' bodies is important to some parents, while others seem happy to use food as a bargaining tool to keep the kids quiet. Emotionally, a mother is torn between giving a child what is right and what a child wants, we've all witnessed the tantrum by the sweet counter in supermarkets. It's been this concern, with sweets especially, that forced many supermarkets to move them away from a key impulse purchasing position by the tills.

Our obsession with sugar has led to attacks on baby foods. When I worked on the German brand Milupa there was a great deal of media attack about sugars in baby foods. The fact that a mother's milk or any natural fruit contains loads of (natural) sugars, or that sugar is a vital element in growth, seems to be ignored. Instead over emotive campaigns control the agenda, forcing brands to make irrational decisions, so they look more ethical and responsible.

Recently the pressure group Sustain, (which campaigns for healthier children's food) claimed that a cheeseburger and chocolate biscuits were more nutritious than some food specifically marketed for babies. They cited Farley's Original Rusk as an offender, made by Heinz, claiming it contains more sugar than McVitie's dark chocolate digestives. They also cited Toddler's Own mini cheese biscuits (another

Heinz product), claiming it had more saturated fat per 100 grams than a McDonald's quarter pounder with cheese. Heinz may well revoke these claims but bad PR sticks and influences consumers.

There are many other substances that brands have been forced to change or omit – GM being one. This then gives the impression that one product is more ethical than another, yet the opposite may actually be true. Zero sugar, zero fat food – for baby or adult – may sound healthy and good but it's about as good as feeding plain white bread to ducks; all they get is a full stomach and no nutrients.

For both mothers and brands the dilemma is a tough one, doing 'what we think is right' or doing what 'we're told is right'. As a society we are often poorly educated and informed about the real issues, instead responding emotionally to what can only be called propaganda.

GETTING THE NAME WRONG

Irradiation was a great breakthrough for science and food. It killed the bacteria that made food rot, increasing shelf life and massively reducing waste. But whoever christened the process 'irradiation' should have been shot. The same applies to the term 'Genetically Modified'. As a mother, would you feel comfortable feeding your kids 'irradiated' or 'genetically modified' food?

The name was a disaster and a good example of how words set the agenda, especially when scientists or civil servants are allowed to name things. In another chapter, I cover the issue of language and ethics and how important it is to use the right words. 'Irradiation' is linked instantly to 'radiation'; not a word to be associated with if you're trying to market something in a favourable light. Forget the facts, predictably there was an irrational emotional reaction against it. Uninformed loud voices decried it and consumer pressure killed it off. Had a more consumer positive word been used, we'd probably be throwing away less of that 25% of food (4.1 million tonnes a year) we do at the moment.

DON'T BLAME IT ON THE BURGER

When two girls in the US tried to sue McDonald's for making them fat they lost. Well, no surprise really but then in the US suing seems to be a favourite past-time for some. They could easily have sued a hundred other fast food companies. It's not just the food that makes us fat but the quantity. The girls argued that McDonald's had failed to inform them that their food was fattening. Just how poorly educated are some people? McDonald's argued (and quite rightly) that any fast food needs to be considered within a balanced diet. But the two girls had been eating up to five portions of McDonald's Chicken McNuggets a week for almost 15 years (from 1987 to 2002)! Hardly a balanced diet.

Of course this opens up a debate about labelling. Why doesn't take-away food carry the same information as pack-aged food? If it did, we'd probably all eat out less. If you knew the calories contained in a cheese stuffed thick crust pizza you'd probably think twice. There does seem to be a need for some form of information and education to help consumers make informed decisions about what they eat. Any brand that champions this will have a clear lead on the rest.

It's not just the food industry to blame but the con-sumer; and not just the marketing but social behaviour and cultural habits. Research shows that young people are more likely to smoke if mum and dad do. Have you noticed how many fat kids have fat parents? If you want to change things you need to start with educating parents and society in general. That's the real challenge for both brands and the government when marketing a healthier lifestyle.

HOW TO SELL AN HONEST SNACK

One of my favourite and I think most beautifully packaged products of recent times, is the '100' range from Calories Exactly. Their website is also an example of how to design a good product website.

The firm was started by Jo Beach who got fed up trying to calculate calories on packaging so she made the calorie count the brand. By putting the face of the founder on the packaging and the website, the product became instantly more personable. We trust people far more than brands. It doesn't try and sell itself on organic, natural or any other ethical content but on its plain honesty – this food has 100 calories. As Jo adds, 'Calories Exactly doesn't claim to make you slim, it only claims to help you enjoy doing it'. They have developed a great range of snacks that have a friendly appeal, which are good for you because you know what quantity of calories you are eating, unlike many 'natural' products that contain hidden calories. Best, they don't try to look worthy and apologetic as so many slimming products do. Eating a 99 calorie slimming cereal bar makes anyone feel sad. These look funky and exciting by contrast and put the joy back into food. Consumers no longer expect to suffer in order to live a more healthy and ethical lifestyle. For a mum it's a great product for the lunchbox.

Honesty is a key ethos of ethics and is just as important as organic or Fairtrade to the consumer. Best of all, honesty builds trust and that's the most important element in building any relationship between consumer and brand. The 100 range gives new meaning to the old term 'good old fashioned honest food'.

NOT SO FINGER LICKING GOOD

McDonald's learnt early on when they took legal action against two campaigners that it doesn't pay to upset the general public. It was a classic David and Goliath scenario and in the media David always wins. Since then they've realized that it pays to clean up their act and be more socially responsible. Now I'm not saying McDonald's is above criticism but they are committed to moving in the right direction; making positive changes rather than voicing token words, like so many companies. Actions speak louder than words and in the ethical market, you are judged by what you do, not just what you say.

KFC may be 'finger licking good' according to the marketing, but is it really? It's highly calorific and worse still, its farming methods are questionable. PETA (People for the Ethical Treatment of Animals) launched a massive 'boycott KFC' campaign against its unethical treatment of chickens. Naked women running through the streets with a banner declaring 'NAKED TRUTH: KFC TORTURES CHICKS' is not a bad way to get attention and attention it got. However, the typical loyal KFC customer probably took little notice. PETA claim that 'More than 850 million chickens are tortured and killed each year for KFC' and have produced a horror video, though they quote just 750 million chickens in it (not sure what happened to the other 100 million). In Canada, KFC have backed down and agreed to a more humane treatment of chickens and to provide vegan chicken (it does seem a bit odd that a vegan would even go into a KFC).

In the UK chickens have become central to the debate about animal welfare. TV chefs and moral crusaders Jamie Oliver and Hugh Fearnley-Whittingstall have both filmed programmes highlighting the lack of welfare attributed to the animals we eat. About 16 million chickens a week are

raised for slaughter and more than 90% of those are intensively farmed. Most intensively farmed chickens are slaugh-
tered at five to six weeks compared to free range's, eight
weeks. Tesco sells more intensively reared chickens than
any other retailer, the Co-op more ethical ones. And the
great British chicken sandwich we all love? It isn't really
British at all, considering that 80% of those sold in our
supermarkets are made from imported meat, with much of
it winging its way from Thailand (83 000 tonnes a year).

Hugh Fearnley-Whittingstall and his chicken campaign
shocked the nation and created a noticeable change in
buying behaviour. Few marketing directors could not be
envious of the power and influence exerted by just one
man; higher welfare chicken sales rose as a direct response
to the programme. Waitrose reported an increase in Select
Farm chicken sales by 15% and Free Range sales up 22%
with Organic sales up 39%. Somerfield saw Free Range
poultry sales rise by 50% and Higher Welfare up 40%. As
a result all supermarkets are stocking more ethically sourced
chickens, giving more choice to the consumer. Those who
remain cynical about the desire of the consumer to buy
more ethically and pay more for it have certainly been
proved wrong by the humble chicken.

SUMMARY

It's ironic that all the food that tastes good is unhealthy for
you. And all the healthy food tastes boring. Try convincing
any kid that a carrot is nicer than a chocolate bar, or that
a salad is nicer than chips with ketchup. Health concerns
are something that has been around for generations and
each generation has a new angle on it. Its crossover with
other ethics has created new propositions and new challenges. For a brand entering the market honesty is essential.
Where Calories Exactly is getting it right, when Sunny D

launched it did everything you shouldn't have done. Consumers now put claims to the test, even a lab test, as Ribena found out. Gü, those delicious puddings, makes no ethical claims, it's honest about being an indulgence food, which is fine. Educated consumers can decide how they want to balance their diet, but a deceived consumer can't.

21
SELLING ETHICAL
BEHAVIOUR

AMERICA'S BEST SELLING PRODUCT

The West has an addiction problem; drink, cigarettes and drugs. Apparently the biggest selling FMCG product by value in America isn't Coca-Cola but cocaine (for every dollar spent in fitness centres $19 is spent on cocaine). It's an irony that by comparison to Coke's massive marketing spend, cocaine doesn't have a marketing department; the brand isn't even registered as a trademark and has never spent a dollar on advertising. But everyone knows the brand name. That's the power of word of mouth. Get a product everyone wants and the word spreads. It also has one of the largest and most efficient distribution networks of all.

It's an interesting debate, but I was confronted by one green who argued that heroin was the ultimate fair trade item. Farmers are well rewarded, protected and supported. Everyone in the chain gets paid well. It encourages small social enterprises in poor communities around the world and provides a job for even the most unqualified person. It's a valid argument. Even if it's a Greek argument (arguing black is white) proving only that in the business of ethics what is ethical can depend upon your viewpoint.

AN ETHICAL DILEMMA

It is said that if we invented alcohol today and society had never encountered it before it would be condemned and banned. It would be classed in the same class as heroin. It's both a toxin and highly addictive. It causes violent behaviour and in excess, severe organ damage. It causes weight gain, depression and ill health.

However, it's been around far too long and is too woven into the fabric of our society and almost every other, to be banished. In moderation it's ok but year on year society grows more concerned about excessive consumption, especially by the youth. Interestingly, alcohol consumption by elderly people has also been growing – one brand is even marketed to them, knowing this.

The massive spend behind alcohol just gets bigger, despite the very limp 'please drink responsibly' message tagged onto drink ads, there really is only one agenda – sell more alcohol. Supermarkets aren't helping, many have been criticized for running discount promotions that just encourage excessive consumption. So, with so much money being spent on encouraging us to drink, how can you hope to counter it with just a fraction of the budget of a single lager campaign?

UNHAPPY HOUR – UNSELLING DRUNKEN BRITAIN

In 2004 I worked with the charities Alcohol Concern and Comic Relief (and a coalition of charities) to run a campaign to raise awareness of the problem the UK was facing. We created a strategy (which was integrated into the government's 'Binge Britain' campaign) and a powerful advertising campaign based on pub names that highlighted the dangers of excessive alcohol consumption: IMAGINE BEING AT YOUR OWN LEAVING PARTY WITHOUT KNOWING IT and NOT EVERY HAPPY HOUR ENDS IN A LAUGH. The headlines were supported by facts – 23000 alcohol related violent incidents a week (and they are just the reported ones); 45% of all deaths by fire in the home are related to alcohol; 350 serious sexual assaults a week. The figures are shocking.

The advertising campaign wasn't heavily funded and no one thought for a minute it would influence the consumer – advertising rarely works on deep set social issues like this. It's questionable if the government's drug, drink and sexual health campaigns have really changed behaviour despite millions being spent. But raising the temperature stimulates the media and challenges public opinion, which leads to political change. The campaign's aim was to start the ball rolling – pump priming.

'Binge Britain' was born and for the following year all eyes were on the sorry state of a drunken nation. Endless articles and TV documentaries appeared with interviews with young people boasting proudly about their hammered nights out while shocking the masses.

Across Europe things are getting worse. Germany suffers from a similar problem but why doesn't Spain? There's a different attitude towards drinking and drunkenness in Spain. They still have a great sense of community, largely lost in the UK. Getting drunk in a community brings social condemnation. But in a socially detached society, no one cares. The Spanish also don't drink to get drunk, they drink smaller quantities and pace themselves (though sadly, drunkenness in major cities is growing there too). Who'd have thought a mindset – go out, get drunk – would be one of our biggest exports! But then every weekend we send thousands of drunken ambassadors off on EasyJet and

Ryanair flights to the cities of Europe to show them all how it's done.

THE REBIRTH OF ALE

During 2008 there was a growing alarm directed at supermarkets discounting alcohol, mainly lager, which is cheaper than bottled water. Once an ale drinking nation, lager now dominates the British drinks market, though recently there's been a massive increase in sales of ale – mainly because of supermarkets stocking products and offering bulk deals, three bottles for £4 makes for good value. There's also been a rediscovery of taste and a new trend for drinking real ales has developed.

There are now over 700 breweries in the UK and ales are a growth area which has led to new brews and the growth of organic brews. The number of organic beers being produced by UK brewers is increasing, some are totally organic but many have gone for certification of the contents of their brews. Brands like Duchy are now becoming commonplace on the shelves.

Back in the 1970s it seemed micro breweries and even the family ones would be driven out of the market by large factory produced beers such as Watney's. Most pubs were owned by a few groups that just saw the process of selling beer as bottom line. Thankfully organizations like CAMRA (Campaign for Real Ales – http://www.camra.org.uk) did a brilliant job of raising awareness, gathering support and pressurizing the big corporate brewers to reverse the trend. It proves the power of community over corporation and what can happen when you engage people in an issue that concerns them. At first it was a battle but finally the penny dropped and the big corporate brewers woke up to one simple fact that too many big businesses forget – the customer is king. The 1970s were dominated by a corporate attitude that treated the masses as mules that took what they were given. That has long gone and today the customers are not only in charge but also use their spending power to get their way.

There has been a growth, or regrowth, since the 1970s of micro breweries and small family brewers like Abbott or the Scottish brewer Black Isle Brewery, who use the rather cheesy jingle-like slogan 'Save the planet, drink organic'. Their Yellowhammer brew won best beer at the Soil Association awards 2008 and was described as 'Seductive honeycomb and beeswax scent and taste. Very fine floral palette with a fine faintly muscat scented finish. Admirable and unusual level of complexity, lots of well balanced different notes'. If you want poetry in place of marketing spin, that does it for me.

I spoke to one organic beer brand at the IFE (International Food & Drink Exhibition) several years ago and they confessed that organic was a novelty to many drinkers: 'It helps make the brew stand out on the shelf but we don't believe it's the primary reason they buy it. They buy it because it tastes so damn good'. Honest at least.

Organic is probably a more natural fit with ale because of its association with quality and taste. There are some organic lagers about as well but ale is a more mature, older drinker's tipple, whereas lager is associated with the youth and is less sophisticated.

The ethical labelling of beer can serve to compliment and validate the consumer's choice. It's like any quality product which we prefer to select rather than grab off the shelves. Consumers like to think that they are making a selection through expertise, judgement and experience. The value and quality of the product reflects upon their own self image and values. I'm the same when I buy beers. I don't drink a lot but I do like to buy quality ale and enjoy it. If I see an unfamiliar brand I'll examine it and maybe buy it. For others it's a wine or whisky. And if there was ever a bunch of drinkers that claim expertise in product selection it's whisky drinkers.

There seems little attempt by spirits companies to market based on ethics. There are a small number of organic whisky brands such as 'Benromach' and 'Highland Harvest' but the whisky is sweeter and less harsh because the process of making organic whisky uses natural yeast instead of cultivated yeast. As a result it's a different product so is unlikely to compete against other whiskies. You can get organic and fair trade rums, 'Papagayo'; vodkas, 'Utkins' and gin, 'Juniper Green'. Though in the case of gin, it's the juniper, coriander, angelica root and savory that are organic. For vodka it's organic grain. It's probably only a matter of time before there are many more options in spirits. For whisky the idea sits nicely against the way whisky is made; its values of sourcing the right ingredients, the right water and the importance of a value driven process. But if it fails on taste it fails in the market.

There's an irony in all things ethical if you look hard. The main organic ingredient in beer is hops. These are not easy to grow organically in the UK so many are now imported. This of course would raise issues with those who oppose food being transported because of the carbon footprint. No matter what you do there's always a balance to strike. But to be honest, if one beer said 'organic' and the other 'low carbon footprint', which sounds the tastier? I really doubt that the latter would sell.

WHY THE WINE INDUSTRY HAS LESS BOTTLE

Alcohol can be divided crudely into two areas of consumption; stuff to drink because it is booze and a drink that you appreciate. The average consumer has become far more educated both in terms of knowledge and palate about wine. Even small supermarkets now display an impressive range of wines and it's no longer acceptable to turn up with cheap plonk at a dinner party.

Wine still remains more sophisticated than cheap lager, but unlike lager, it's been making an effort to become more environmentally friendly (even if transport is a big issue). The issue the wine industry faces, unlike the ale industry, is the great distance heavy loads of wine and its bottles have to travel. However, by putting wine in lighter bottles (and even plastic ones) CO_2 emissions have been reduced by 28000 tonnes over the past three years, which is the equivalent of taking 8500 cars off the road. If every producer or retailer swapped to lighter packs the wine industry could save over 990000 tonnes of CO_2 annually. And due to its long shelf life wine can opt for slower and more environmentally friendly methods of transport, such as boats, as opposed to planes.

I believe that the badge of organic and Fairtrade does offer the consumer a value added choice and makes you look more caring if you take one of those bottles to a dinner party. But I doubt the public gets really excited about the CO_2 issue, especially as it's only reducing an issue and not removing it. If you cared that much you'd drink water instead. There are bigger issues, such as recycling or the effects upon the cork industry since artificial corks were introduced.

THE REBIRTH OF CIDER

Cider has seen a massive revival; lighter and sweeter than lager it's become a popular and trendy drink in bars. The trend started in Scotland and soon spread, fuelled by a massive marketing and advertising campaign for the C&C Group owned brand Magners (the product is sold under the Bulmers brand in Ireland). Using its Irish heritage, Magners has grown rapidly over the last five years to become the number one packaged cider brand in Great Britain. The brand has extended to 17 markets around the world, including Spain, Germany and the US, a truly great example of effective marketing at work (the same couldn't be said for a number of other C&C brands). Magners was originally developed by Stuart Wootten (export director) who saw that the international growth of Irish pubs provided a natural market for an indigenous Irish cider.

However, it's not selling on its ethics and there are no claims about organic apples or fair trade. It's selling heritage, quality and lifestyle with a hint of local community. Using 'time' as a theme it emphasises the time it takes to make with slogans like 'All in its own Good Time' and then reflects on the time you can take to enjoy it. Would it sell any better if real ethical values were overlaid? It may sell a few extra bottles to more conscientious consumers but Magners/Bulmers is after a mass market, so it has to deliver against the average desires of consumers.

THE AVERAGE CONSUMER PURCHASING ATTITUDE

If you consider that consumers can vary their buying behaviour between being passionate about why and what they buy (this covers not just ethical consumers but those who buy on quality, specialism and the exotic) and (at the other end) concern with convenience and price. We all behave this way, depending on circumstances, environment and needs. What you get in the middle is an average behaviour, the Average Consumer Purchasing Attitude.

This is what mass market brands go after. That's why organic ciders, beers and lagers sell in lesser quantities. But as a society becomes more conscientious, as it has in some markets, the ACPA moves across the line. During a recession, in many markets price becomes a key factor and it moves the other way. It should be noted that during a recession conscientious buying can also increase.

Supermarkets selling bulk discounted lager encourage people to buy with less concern for either taste or ethics. Four bottles of lager for the price of one ale challenges anyone. However, as most of us have learnt a £10 bottle of wine reduced to £5 is really a £5 bottle that's been sold at £10.

ACPA

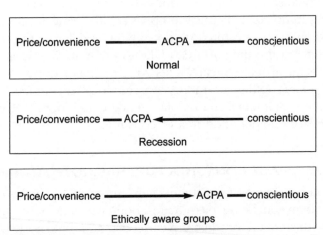

Figure 21.1 Average consumer purchasing attitude

LOCAL AND ORGANIC MARKETING

The 'local' element is also becoming a marketing plus. Small local micro breweries are much more attractive and romantic than large brewers' factories. The idea of supporting the small guy seems very positive and community focussed. There's even an element in this in Bulmers marketing, do you think of big factory-like brewery or some romantic Irish brew house?

'Organic' adds to the romantic image and brings to mind woodcuts of farmers in hop fields and old corn barrows. It highlights the ingredients and totally ignores the fact that alcohol is one of the most dangerous chemicals around. Which makes for an irony – the idea that most people hold about organic is that it's chemical free. Think about it.

But there are two other key issues with drinks. First taste; no one will drink organic, fair trade local beer if it doesn't taste great. Good ales and wines are taste dominant products. The second is price. There's one over priced organic brand that's gone into ales and personally, I found the product to be average and the price tag too high, leaving it to sit more comfortably in the gift section. No matter what the ethical claims may be, they can't be a substitute for crap.

A WORLD OF TOO MUCH CONSUMER CHOICE

We are big consumers of wine and drink a diverse range of the red, white and pink stuff. It's big business. France exported over 5.3 million tonnes in 2006, Italy 4.7 and Spain over 3.6. In comparison with the post-war period of the late 1940s and early 1950s we now have so much choice. As consumers we like the idea of choice but hate it in reality. That is, in part, the basis of branding; we like others to choice edit for us. We want convenience because most of us have little time and it's just too much brain ache. Just try this simple experiment; try shopping in a Chinese supermarket (unless you are Chinese). It's a mind blowing experience. Trying to read every pack, trying to work out what everything is and the difference between the red box and green box. Even if you are just buying 20 items it makes it very stressful.

Ethics has added yet another layer to the many factors we have to choose from; organic, fair trade, local, lower carbon footprint, and the rest. As if picking a wine wasn't hard enough already. The shortcut is to build a strong brand, like Duchy, that captures all the values. (In another chapter I talk about the choice hierarchy and how brands need to influence it and suppress lesser choices.) The deeply conscientious consumer will take time to 'look behind the label' but the masses won't. They prefer to pass the responsibility over to others, part of the success of the M&S campaign – you shop, they sort out the ethics.

SUMMARY

It's somewhat ironic that an industry that causes endless diseases and deaths has an ethical pitch. People will always abuse themselves, history tells us that, so at least what they take may as well be as ethical as possible. Proving that there's hypocrisy in how people buy based on ethics.

22
FROM BRAND VALUES
TO BRAND VALUE

BBC SELLS DISGUSTING FOOD

Does your message have both value and values? Value has always been defined as what you get for your money, not just price. A quality hemp t-shirt at £20 is better value than a cheap one at £4 if it lasts 10 times longer (though try telling Primark customers that).

As the credit crunch settles into a recession many brands are abandoning values for cheapness. A 50p apple pie is probably not going to be as nice as a £2 one. In fact, what people get away with is quite shocking. Few of us are aware of what we're really eating. Recently, I was involved in the making of a BBC programme, 'Mischief', which set out to educate us on the ethics of what actually goes into some of our food.

The programme created the most disgusting meat and fruit pies that fell within EC regulations. The fruit pie had about 20% fruit and was largely bulked out with corn starch (wallpaper paste). The meat pie had God knows what in it. The aim was to whistle blow on how you can make something so awful look appealing and good. We decided on using heritage, personal identity and a few wild claims. It was funny, featuring the comedian Alex Riley and proved that looking ethical is not the same as being ethical. Unfortunately, too many packaging spin doctors are doing just that.

Heritage is great, because it taps into ideas we hold in our own head, without having to define anything. Words like 'traditional' imply trust and quality, even though this may not necessarily be the case. By association we create a romantic image of a healthy, wholesome and hearty 'traditional' way of life.

Putting a name to a brand also works to make us think that it's been made by a person who is passionate and cares about the food. Has anyone met Mr Kipling? Of course not because there isn't a Mr Kipling; it was created in 1967 by Rank Hovis McDougall (now owned by Premier Foods) in order to develop the packaged cake market. But we, the buying cake-eating public, have an image of a friendly local baker. Far from the reality of a large modern factory churning out mass produced 'exceedingly good cakes'. The company's reply to the question 'is Mr Kipling real?' is 'he exists in the hearts and minds of our employees and customers'.

Tom Caxton Traditional Best Bitter Home Brew is another false identity. The story goes that the agency working on naming this new product sent a memo to the client with a list of final names they'd selected. The client didn't like the names at all. The memo was signed by the agency account handler, Tom Caxton. The rest is home brewing history. There are many more ...

So for the BBC TV programme, we used Alex's dad and named the pies Mr Riley's Pies (eat your heart out Mr Kipling!) A few nice old graphics, some paper wrapping and we were almost there. Just a few claims needed. We couldn't say it was organic, fair trade or even farm fresh, but it was dolphin friendly and didn't have any GM in it.

WHEN A BRAND BECOMES A TURKEY

You'll have to excuse the pun in the title but I do work in advertising, though we like to use the term 'wordplay'. To put distance between itself and its recent bad publicity and in order to look more ethical, Bernard Matthews have repackaged themselves as Bernard Mathews Farms with a nice weathercock logo so as to give you a sense of the countryside (shouldn't that be a weather turkey?). The ads feature an employee, like Guy the turkey farmer, or Ian and Kevin, all holding a placard declaring how proud they are to work for Bernard Matthews and how all of their birds are home grown '100% British turkeys'.

The company has been through a chequered period. It received bad PR when two employees were seen using a turkey as a baseball bat. Then there was the bird flu issue and numerous revelations and accusations about exploited workers, unfit conditions, animal cruelty, low hygiene levels, battery farming and injecting substances into the meat. Some were untrue but once the press get going, the truth is the first victim. The website does make a good effort to dispel the myths and convey the company's values, although I doubt many consumers ever visit sites like these.

They even tried to push Mr Matthews (famous for his 'bootiful' ads of the 1980s) out of retirement to front a defensive press ad campaign, but the damage (rightly or wrongly) was done and ticked about every unethical box going. Their new positioning is an attempt to play off several positive ethical values. Local – 'all our turkeys are home grown'. The addition of the 'farms' is a nod to nature and a more traditional way of life. 'Pride' communicates an ethos that the company really cares and portrays a more human/personable side to the business (rather than faceless corporation). To give the business a human face was a successful move but over the last 10 years, Bernard Matthews has become just another faceless, meat packaging company.

Has the Bernard Matthews brand been seriously, if not permanently, damaged? I suggested to its previous agency that they should grow a new brand, perhaps play off the American love of turkey and do an American themed range; it would be cheaper than trying to keep on old one on a life support system. But companies often get attached to old brands even when it's better to move on. And there's no lack of research groups who will tell you that the public have an emotional attachment to the brand. Well, until they can buy another version cheaper.

Brands are like people and when something unpleasant is revealed about them, we don't forget it. No matter how hard I try and buy the new image, when I look at a pack of turkey, all those negative images prevail. It'll take a generation to move beyond the bad publicity and even then, word of mouth can keep a bad story alive.

Karen Fraser, one of the leading experts on brands and ethics, publishes the Ethical Brand Index. One of the things she highlights is the 'conflicted consumer': '1 in 4 shoppers are "conflicted consumers". Though they may look like loyal customers, they are ready to switch brands if a more ethical alternative becomes available'. This could be an issue for Bernard Matthews; their image has been damaged by what some may call unethical practices, and even though there may not be many highly ethical alternatives, being deemed to be less ethical than even the supermarket own brands, doesn't do well for sales.

BRANDING MR RILEY'S PIES

Back to the BBC programme on disgusting food. With the aid of a few gimmicks and traditional values we had packaged a totally disgusting and unethically produced product so as to look delicious and tasty. Surprisingly, they actually did taste good.

The programme makers managed to mix humour with some shocking facts regarding just how much rubbish goes into our food, i.e. the addition of water and chemicals in order to add weight and volume. It is worrying but somehow the humour kept you watching. I've always argued that humour is a great way to put across dramatic and shocking facts because it lowers the defensiveness of people. Comedian Mark Thomas (who's just written a book on how bad Coke is) has used humour to great effect to expose many unethical issues. He even used a group of school kids to set up an arms dealing company in order to expose the practice. Michael Moore has less of a stand-up technique but adopts a light-hearted approach, and often bizarre methods, to get attention.

WHEN IS FOOD DISGUSTING?

One of the questions raised by the programme was 'what is defined as disgusting?' In the comfortable West we can afford to use only the best cuts of meat but if you're a poor family in Africa, every bit of an animal will be used. Far from disgusting, with a different paradime, you see things as anything but disgusting. In a strange kind of way the programme highlighted how spoilt we are in the West. These pies may be disgusting to us but to a starving child they are actually good food.

SUMMARY

The food industry has a long way to go to be truly ethical. Processed foods are big business and while packaging in supermarkets has to carry essential information about content, fast foods and food sold through the food services industry don't. But does the public care? This is a debatable issue but I think many separate the two, knowing that life is about a balance of good and bad. Certainly more of us are looking for the better option but sometimes there is no option. Thankfully most of us don't know what is in some of the food we eat. But then again perhaps we are all being too middle class about some food, moved more by perceptions than facts.

23
FAST FASHION

THE HIERARCHY OF ETHICS

Fashion is a dubious business. From debates surrounding size zero models, sweat shops, animal abuse (the skinning of animals alive) and the use of chemicals in cotton, few industries have suffered so much negative publicity. And when it's not being beaten up in the press over its ethics it's mocked for its shallowness, ridiculous designs and false lifestyle. Fashion as a brand has not been well managed over the years.

There is probably no other industry in such an ethical conflict as the fashion industry. One part is championing ethics with innovation and passion, the other exploiting millions in sweat shops across the world in order to feed the desire for cheap fashion.

It is equally divided over which ethics are better than others, saving the planet or saving people? There are an estimated 40 million workers, mostly female, in the global textile trade who work long hours for poor wages, in unsafe working conditions. They are often abused, harassed and are given no rights. Just so we in the West can have cheap clothes.

The debate over helping people in Africa, Asia and South America is a complicated one. Whereas fairly traded clothes may support small communities, some argue that even if large producers are running sweat shops they are offering a better life than starvation and utter poverty to hundreds of thousands of families, something fair trade can't. There's no doubt that without our hunger for fashion there would be more hunger in the world.

The pressure on retailers to produce cheaper fashion fast means that many step beyond the line. Primark was revealed to be using three Indian companies who were subcontracting work out to companies that used child labour. It is ironic that the youth of today are supporting (even if exploited) the youth of the Third World.

Meanwhile environmentalists want to slow churn and create a more sustainable industry encouraging longer life, more repair, recycling and remaking. They want to see less seasonal change and a change in values.

Then there's the whole social issue surrounding the size zero debate. It seems that in today's society kids are brainwashed into believing that thinness equates automatically with beauty and success. The Dove 'respect' campaign has raised this issue in the US.

The TNS Worldpanel Fashion puts people issues ahead of the environment but given the choice of a great looking shoe that's unethical versus a dull looking ethical one, just how ethically orientated is the consumer? They claim that the ethical priority is: 1) no sweatshops; 2) no child labour; 3) a decent wage; and 4) no environmental damage.

But we Brits love to shop and where there's money there's exploitation. So can we ever achieve a happy balance? I really doubt it but there's a lot further that we could go towards a better deal for both people and the planet. What seems to determine the hierarchy of ethics is the media. What they write becomes the issue of the moment. It's a sad thought that a journalist can direct such a shallow industry.

THE POWER OF THE HIGH STREET

Thankfully there's been a growing interest in ethical fashion but the key to making it the norm is to break into the big high street chains. According to the TNS Worldpanel Fashion's annual ethical clothes report, almost half of UK consumers felt ethics were an important factor when choosing clothing and footwear. But the ethical fashion industry is small and made up of small producers, with little power and no economy of scale. Big retailers need low prices and besides exploiting people, mass production does lower costs.

Many brands focus on using environmental fabrics and ensuring that workers are not abused. But if it looks dull, it'll take more than ethics to shift it. And if it's not fashionable no high street store will even look at it. I believe, given the way high street chains work: the logistics, design to shop time and the need to have a supply that can be turned on or off like a tap, it's a challenge for any ethical fashion brand. The future lies in the mass of small independents and online. Brands like Adili, who have a range that rivals Next and M&S, have proven that online is a place to be. The savings on retail units means that prices are more competitive.

Of course, what makes fashion ethical depends on who's defining it; you, the brand or the public? Adili provides this as their ethical check list: Fairtrade, alternative fibres, recycled, organic, traditional skills, locally sourced, lower environmental impact, supporting charitable projects, working conditions and labour standards. They go on to define those ethical bullet points: 'Fair trade is a trading partnership based on dialogue, transparency and respect that seeks greater equity in international trade. It contributes to sustainable development by offering better trading conditions to, and securing the rights of, marginalised producers and workers'.

Some of these points you may not have considered but all have a value that could be marketed and would fit well within a fashion version of the Ethical Sphere.

ETHICAL FASHION WEEK

Ethical fashion, or 'eco-sustainable fashion' as it's now called by some, is a growing category dominated by small producers and suppliers, who are passionate and dedicated to the cause of ethics. Although there are still those trading in ethnic clothing many are producing cutting edge designs such as Terra Plana and Junky Styling. People Tree smartened up their designs (one of the original ethical fashion brands) and managed to grab a concession in Top Shop – a token attempt by Green's empire to look ethical. I was surprised to see that when Top Shop launched the Kate Moss range no emphasis was given to ethics. In the world of fashion marketing celebrities have a big influence on the buying public. Would anyone have queued for Moss's range if it had no celebrity association? For all the words of encouragement the ethical fashion industry still needs some top names to support it and wear it. Just as Julia Roberts and the Hollywood pack sold the Prius, if a small number of top celebrities pulled together, they could raise the profile of ethics in the fashion world so as to become an accepted and desirable fixture.

London Fashion Week, exciting for some, amusing for others, has become a great platform for the alternative ethical fashion movement, especially Estethica, to market itself. Adili, the leading online fashion retailer, sponsored the 'Make Your Mark In Fashion' event aimed at finding young designers. Junky Styling also sponsor a young designers event. The event has provided greater exposure for many of the ethical brands at the designer end of the market and now more and more of these brands are linking up with fashion colleges and thus influencing young designers.

Even though the price for catwalk success is high and a barrier to small ethical fashion producers, it could also be seen as a welcome escape, from the pompous superficiality of the high end fashion market. Personally, I'd rather see an Edinburgh Fringe style of event; it feels more honest. It's hard to be taken seriously as an ethical fashion label if you become shallow.

SAVING THE PLANET, ONE STEP AT A TIME

According to one survey carried out by a leading shoe brand across Europe, women claim that they consider the ethical implications when buying a product, much more so than men. In reality it's the other way round. Men's ethical purchasing is closer to their claims while women are more easily distracted by the 'wow I really must have those shoes' factor. 'Let's be honest', commented one friend of mine. 'If you want to save the planet shoes are not the place to start'. I'd disagree. Buy a decent pair of shoes and walk everywhere. It's a start.

Shoes are essential to all of us, and some would argue that having 20 pairs to match any choice of clothing is essential as well. But it's not an area that has really turned itself towards saving either the planet or people. When I worked with Rieker (a German shoe company) I suggested that they should be the first large brand to launch an ethical shoe. It was over a year later before any big brand did so. There are many small brands in the market offering stylish, reasonably priced ethical shoes such as Worn Again, Vivo, Terra Plana and People Tree. Gone are the days when the only ethical shoes were either clogs or straw sandals.

The challenge for all areas of the fashion industry is that design and aesthetics comes first and ethics second. No one wants to look bad: 'if I'm going to save the planet, I'm going to save it in style', was the comment of one young girl I questioned as she left the Terra Plana shop in Covent Garden (we were doing some research prior to proposing a campaign for Vivo).

SMALL THINGS CAN MAKE A BIG DIFFERENCE

Many ethical fashion brands just don't have the budget to make big claims. Instead they are being more innovative by making small significant changes.

Howies (the ethical clothing company set up by two ex Saatchi people and bought by Timberland) has a novel approach to the usual shoot on a hot palm beach. They sent their new fashion lines in the post to friends in hot places and got them to model them and send back the photos. More eco-friendly than sending a dozen glam models out by plane but a lot less fun. They also claim to be able to make repairs which extend the life of their product.

Patagonia used a nut from the rainforest as a button. They tested a sample, washing them 50 times before making and selling a lot of shirts. But customers started returning the shirts with broken buttons. This was a mystery; they'd passed the test, so why had they broken? It seems that the washing and drying process recreated the same conditions within the rainforest – of a wet period followed by sunshine. The seed pods/nuts were programmed to break open in order to let the seed out. Sometimes the environment isn't your best friend.

THE TRUE PRICE OF COTTON

Cotton may sound harmless but it's not so white. It uses 25% of all insecticides and 10% of all pesticides, yet accounts for just 3% of the world's agriculture. And according to the World Health Organization toxic pesticides in some cottons are killing 20 000 farmers a year and the dyes are polluting water supplies. Not only that, the average shirt uses 4000 litres of water from start to finish. So, as a market now worth over $2 billion, cotton is posing quite a few dilemmas for the conscientious consumer.

Most organic cotton comes from Turkey, China and India but a few critics question the validity of some sources of organic cotton, suspecting that more is sold under the organic umbrella than actually produced. Consumers are advised to stick to major trusted brands.

The BBC produced a great programme which was definitely worth watching, called the 'The True Price of Cotton', which tracked its value from the field to the shop. Not surprisingly, most of the sale value of a t-shirt goes into the retailer's pockets.

THE DEVIL WEARS PRIMARK

Primark and other cheap fashion shops love the credit crunch and are set to dominate the high street with their 'fast fashion' approach for quite a while. Providing credit crunched consumers with clothes so disposable they're not worth washing may be good for bank balances but not the environment. Our cheap fashion thrills are causing a major landfill problem – 74% of clothes bought are thrown away; that's 7.5 billion items of clothing going into our bins annually in the UK, accounting for up to 30% of all waste sent to landfill (and the government is worried about direct mail which comprises less than 2% of household waste). Of course, we could all put them into bags and send them to the developing world, except that when they get there many are sold and not given away, which puts local people out of business. It's shocking how many crooks will jump on the ethical bandwagon in order to make a quick buck.

There is a small movement which adapts clothes from Primark; students creatively customizing cheap, plain t-shirts and shirts to sell to friends and in markets. How ironic, that a young person in the West can make more money from adapting one Primark item, than a factory worker will probably get for making a hundred. In a strange way Primark are actually helping lower income people in the West enjoy reasonable clothing. A factor Wal-Mart has used in the US to sell at its low prices, helping the family get more value for their dollar.

'The Devil wears Primark' was the title of damning BBC 'Panorama' programme about the queen of fast fashion. No retailer has managed to draw so much flak and so many customers at the same time. Some see Primark as the hypocrisy of the consumer who one minute claims to value ethics but then shops in Primark: 'We all have our price and if it's low enough we'll trade in our values for a t-shirt', was one comment that I wrote in a blog. Is Primark the devil or does it take two to tango? Would they survive if we all believed in buying only ethically? It's easy to blame the retailer but in a quote I used from the 'V is for Vendetta' film (for an Action Aid viral for 'Who Pays?'): 'if you want to know who is really to blame, you only need to look in a mirror'.

From a marketing perspective, it's not as though Primark spends millions on marketing. They don't need to when they have word of mouth and fashion magazines. And their formula is simple; reasonable quality, good looking but dirt cheap.

However, fashion is fickle and moves like the wind. If wearing Primark became unfashionable, as it could easily do, all the youth would shop elsewhere. This is the danger of being linked to a social network, it can change direction. With a growing trend towards a more conscientious clothes shopper, Primark needs to be wary.

Remember, Woolworth's was once everyone's favourite cheap store!

If I were Primark I would engage my consumer, especially the under 25s, and set up a consumer panel in order to demonstrate that I was listening. I'd invest in more visible ethical values and products. I'd look to be more innovative than just organic mixed cotton (which can have just 2.5% organic cotton in it). I'd look at how they could deliver value and ethics in the long term. I would perhaps take over factories in the developing world, build homes and hospitals and manage every part of the process, similar to the flower industry in Kenya and to what Cadbury's did in the past. This also takes out the biggest problem in the ethical supply chain – the middle man – who is often the first to exploit those in a weak position. I'd build a strong emotional relationship with my customer based on more than just cheap prices. I'd invest in a more positive brand reputation. I'd hire a Kate Moss equivalent and launch an ethical fashion range, working to support smaller brands as well. I'd pay the workers more. I'd make ethics the new fashion. Brands come and go and even the most successful can fall, how often have the post mortems said, 'if only they'd done this when they were at the top'.

According to TNS Worldpanel Fashion under 25s are the least likely to buy ethical fashion – with 60% buying what they like and want regardless of ethical positioning; hence, why Primark does so well with the young. Yet despite these statistics, there is evidence to the contrary, suggesting that the youth are more motivated by ethical issues and more environmentally aware than ever before. The internet has exposed them to the truth of what's happening in the world and they don't like it. If I was a politician I'd be very cautious about the coming generation, no other has had so much information and can wield so much power and influence.

At my daughter's school, a group of kids who were passionate about Fairtrade wanted to start a stall selling Fairtrade snacks. They were told they couldn't because the school had signed a deal with the snack machine contractor forbidding it. Furious one teenager addressing the Head replied, 'you may have signed it, but we, the pupils didn't'. From that day on the machines (selling Nestlé chocolate) were jammed up and it became unacceptable to buy from them. It only takes one person and a social network to start a revolution.

'HOW DO THEY MAKE 'EM SO CHEAP?'

I was on a bus in North London; two teen girls with large Primark bags sat behind me and a smart man in his early forties reading 'The Guardian' stood beside me. One girl said to the other 'Err, it's amazing, I dunno 'ow they can make a t-shirt so cheap'. Her mate chewed her gum and looked blankly at her friend. 'It's simple', commented 'The Guardian' reading man, who'd overheard the comment. 'Girls of your age work in sweatshop factories in the Third World for up to 12 hours a day in unpleasant conditions, with few breaks and for less than £1.50 a day'. The gum chewing teenager looked at him. There was pause. 'Where's the Third World?' she replied.

In fact the average is £1 a day and some high street brands have been paying as little as just 60 p.

HOW SPAIN IS CONQUERING THE HIGH STREET

It seems that the nation which is mostly making its mark on the UK and European high street is Spain, with brands like Mango, Hoss, Zara and Desigual. Zara has brought affordable fashion to the masses, much to French Connection's disadvantage.

Desigual and Hoss are two brands with strong ethical values. Hoss began with the ethos to support the homeless (originally the name was 'Homeless' and written in short as 'Ho-ss') but instead of launching as a worthy brand with small shops, they went straight upmarket and opened their first store in the most high end fashionable area of Madrid, Serrano. Hoss aren't cheap but even though they don't market it as a value, they still support the homeless.

Desigual, my favourite fashion brand, have become the next natural brand after Mambo and All Saints. Their clothes are unique and they have helped many young designers get a foot on the ladder. Helping young people may seem like a lesser ethical value than fair trade or environmentalism, but to the consumer helping young people get started is seen as a positive and ethical benefit to society. The assumption that ethics is all about saving something or someone has been disproven by Desigual, who have tapped into the movement of buying local and supporting local traders. On the Geography Of Ethics chart that I use, it falls close to home, which is where both charity and ethics start from.

DON'T LOOK BEHIND THE LABEL, LOOK AT IT

What is lacking in the retail sector is clear honest labelling. Consumers want to know what they are buying. You shouldn't have to look 'behind the label' (to quote Stuart Rose) but at the label. Consumers also need to be made more aware of the different ethical factors that can help them decide. There's a big need for education. But this all needs to be done without ending up in the mess the food industry created. As I keep saying, there is no one ethical consumer type, but many. I've used the polar positioning of people versus planet, from fair trade to environmental issues, to make marketers think more about different values.

We have to accept that some will be those who are interested mainly in organic hemp, others mainly in the treatment of the workers; but even then, there will be a folio of ethical values embodied within the consumer. Add to that the many other factors you could bring in and you can see why you need a model like the Ethical Sphere to help you get it right.

The label is a powerful marketing tool, we know that up to 75% of decision making in supermarkets is at point of sale, so I would imagine it's almost 95% in fashion. At that key moment of decision making a stronger set of ethical values could swing the deal. Indecision is a problem when picking which boots or dress or jeans to buy; sales assistants know all too well that their main role is to aid decision making, so why not use the label to do it for you?

SUMMARY

The consumer is torn between ethics, design and price. Primark will be successful because it will do whatever it has to in order to keep prices low. Ethical fashion simply cannot compete against low price. But it can compete on design, quality and therefore value. Traditionally, ethical fashion has been dull in design but a new generation of designers and brands are changing that. There will always be the two ends of the scale sitting next to each other in the high street, but for those entering the ethical fashion arena design and quality are vital and come before ethics. Most people won't buy an outfit that looks bad, no matter how ethical it is.

24
WASHING GREEN

THE GREAT CLEANING LIE

Where once we used simple things such as lemon juice, vinegar and soapy water to clean our homes we now use an army of products. The cleaning market is big business and a business that has grown off our paranoia about germs. The trouble is that our homes are actually too clean, which means that kids grow up with little exposure to normal bacteria and become ill easily. When my daughter spent five months in Africa on a VSO trip the first thing they were told was that they'd all get ill within the first few days because we live in too sterile an environment. Nature is a good protector and you need exposure to build up immunity.

TV ads have for years been a propaganda machine for chemical companies to sell us a mass untruth – our homes are full of dangerous bacteria. We are shown animated monsters lurking in drains and the toilet and work surfaces harvest deadly bacteria. Your family are under threat. What you must have is a cupboard of chemicals that can kill 99% of all known germs, which is a dubious claim in itself.

A recent ad (that now includes the flu virus within its list of things it kills) shows a mum cleaning a surface and then a kid licking up sandwich filling that has dropped onto the table top. This is trying to portray an image of cleanliness but the reality is that kid's food now has a load of chemicals on it.

The truth is, your sink cupboard, which will contain at least six chemical cleaners, should carry a chemical hazard warning sign on it. If you measured the air after a morning's cleaning it would probably be declared a danger zone, yet multi million pound marketing budgets have sold us a false image; well, that's the power of TV advertising. By including scents like pine, lavender and rose in these cleaners we now have emotional evidence that our homes are cleaner.

By contrast, the environmentally friendly cleaning market is still very small and the brands don't have the budget to counter the big chemical companies who have a lot of Mr Muscle. Even getting into the supermarkets, who prefer to support the larger groups like P&G, Unilever, Johnson & Johnson, Colgate and Palmolive, is tough and often expensive. For one brand entering the UK market, selling their product as a supermarket's own label was the only economically viable way to get on the shelf. The smart supermarkets have seen the eco-ethical market as a good one for their own label as it makes the brand look good.

The alternative is to have a celebrity branded product like Fresh & Green, which is TV chef Anthony Worral Thompson's own range of environmentally friendly cleaners. 'Tough on dirt, gentle on the planet' is the brand's strap line. The range is endorsed by the WWF and produced by Organica. The product is environmentally friendly, contains no harmful chemicals and is derived from natural plant extracts using sustainable agricultural practices. As a cleaner it won best buy in 'Which?' magazine in 2007. Organica are an amazing company and supply natural products to the agriculture, horticulture, aquaculture, retail, industrial and wastewater sectors.

SOAP POWDERS, FRIEND OR FOE?

Britain uses on average 150 litres of water per head per day (report by Waterwise and Ariel in February 2008). If we all stopped using pre-wash on our washing machines we could save 6 billion litres of water per year. If we only washed a full load we could save 608 million litres a week nationally. And then there's all that electricity we use.

Whereas soap powder has for a long while been a topic of environmental concern with images of rivers full of foam, algae blooms and dying fish, somehow the far more lethal chemicals we pour down our sinks and toilets have escaped the debate.

Environmentally friendly detergents were some of the very first green products on supermarket shelves. Ecover, launched in 1980, marketed themselves on 'zero phosphates' and biodegradability.

I recall an ethical product that was launched in the late 1980s at the same time as Unilever's Radion brand. The two couldn't have been more opposite. One marketed itself on its environmental claims while Radion, a name designed deliberately to create a suggestion of power like radiation, marketed itself on brutal cleaning power and its smell. The packaging was bright orange and lurid. Sod green, the average housewife wanted cleaner whites (even if we wear very few white clothes these day). White is a symbol of purity and the detergent industry has always used it as a benchmark to define the quality of cleaning whilst encouraging the notion that anything less than brilliant white means you are a bad wife and mother.

Radion's sales rocketed, backed by a massive but very bad TV advertising campaign, featuring home movies. The product was also big on fragrance, which ended up with a bizarre campaign that featured bus tickets impregnated with the smell. Despite a good launch its sales settled at just 2%

(compared to Persil's 28%) and it was killed off in a brand cull in 1990.

The ethical product relied on PR and word of mouth. In the beginning it looked good for the supermarkets to stock it but Radion was a bigger seller and so got more shelf space and greater prominence.

TURN TO 30

However, the debate about detergents has moved on, now that most mainstream brands are less environmentally damaging and energy consumption has become the big environmental debate. Ariel's 'turn to 30' campaign is pure genius, saving up to 40% of energy. P&G have created a 'Do a good turn' (a good pun) campaign that encourages people to spread the word and pushes the point that we are currently wasting £7.5 billion worth of energy a year in the UK alone – that's the equivalent to £125 per person. But their website is dull and clumsy and far too wordy and factual, though I'm sure the client loved it, even down to the clichéd wind turbines (intended to symbolize doing a good turn).

Not only does Ariel's partnership with consumers make a difference, especially when encouraging them to tell their friends to do a good turn as well, but it also leaves them thinking that the product must be a good cleaner at that temperature. More recently they have overlaid a charitable campaign for African clean water projects, adding the people dimension.

WASH AT ZERO

Recently Ariel has launched an even lower temperature powder, Ariel Excel Gel Bio, which washes at just 15 degrees, and there are even products claiming to wash at zero degrees. I think this may be going too far, though the Australians have had one for a while. As a consumer, 30 degrees I can buy but zero leaves me unconvinced and challenges that part of my mind that's been brainwashed into thinking you have to wash things brilliantly white in order to be a good person. I also wonder just what they have to put in it to make it work at a zero temperature. I have a feeling it won't hit the sales targets and will vanish off the shelves in time, though I'm happy to be proved wrong. There is one slight problem – my washing machine doesn't have a zero degree programme. Of course, all of this is irrelevant if you have a tumble dryer.

Even though the agenda has shifted, new labels are entering the market through online retailers, such as the Aquados Simple range. This is the first UK laundry product to carry the EU Eco-label, something that few consumers have any awareness of. Labelling can be a great marketing device but with so many labels already (and a few dubious ones) being one of the few brands in this category that has been awarded it sadly carries little weight with the consumer. The Grocer magazine report last year highlighted how confusing labelling is, with few consumers really knowing what they mean, and so finding it easier to simply ignore them.

Even though the Simple product is well packaged, so many products in the ethical cleaning sector look dull and worthy. For many brands their packaging is weak and their website too anal. When will green brands wake up and take a leaf out of the big brands' book and invest in good packaging, good websites and a good brand positioning? It's just as important as the product, staff, offices and the telephone. It seems that many green brands see branding, marketing and design as a cost and not an essential investment. They don't need big advertising budgets – remember that up to 85% of purchasing decisions are made at the point of sale. It's not just about getting the product right; you need to get the packaging and the marketing proposition right. If you think it's all about the product, just remember that the average woman spends her money on bad chemicals, sold in a way to make her feel good – that's the power of good marketing!

I made an amusing observation when I was researching laundry products – Sainsbury's online store does give Simple one extra value – under 'dietary information' it lists it as 'suitable for vegans'. A slight oversight I think.

THE BIG SOFTENER CON

One of the great 'do we really need that' products within the cleaning category has to be fabric conditioners. Unknown to the public, these products have grown in size as manufacturers have added more water and put them in bigger containers. With the move back to concentrates (and government pressure to reduce packaging) it allows brands to claim an environmental advantage – less packaging means less waste, less transport and therefore it's good for the planet. Now they don't just care for your clothes but the planet too. Green spin if there ever was.

This is the way of things at the moment, before the product would have been marketed on convenience, smaller containers means less to carry, less space needed under the sink but now brands have woken up to the fact that the consumer sees a value in ethical claims so smaller packaging becomes an environmental claim.

NOT SO CLEAN CLEANERS

Ocado has reported a 60% increase in sales of environmentally friendly household products, which can't be good news for chemical companies, unless you are Clorox and have just expanded into the green market despite being a major manufacturer of bleach based cleaners.

My discovery of just how nasty traditional household cleaners are came when I pitched for an eco-friendly brand that sells well in parts of Europe and Asia but wanted to break into the lucrative UK market – apparently we are one of the biggest buyers of cleaning products.

The products, which I can't name (for reasons of a Non Disclosure Agreement), I shall call 'EnvironCleaner' by way of an example of reframing a product away from the environment.

The owners saw it as an environmentally friendly product; it contained no nasty chemicals and was almost totally natural. From the packaging to the manufacture almost every element was as environmentally friendly as it could be. Given that, surely the marketing plan would be to show lots of lovely clean rivers and images of nature and celebrate its environmentally friendly virtues. But good marketing always looks at options and at the consumer first. Assume nothing, especially in the field of ethical marketing. More people get it wrong than right because they assume too much.

The shocking truth about chemical cleaners is a powerful tool to unseat a market that sees little threat from alternative brands. You only have to tell any man or woman the truth about what he or she is spraying around the home and pouring down the toilet and what it's doing to them and their family and you'll get a shocked reaction. Further, the truth makes them feel that they've been conned (well they have) by the big brands and so trust is destroyed.

The trouble is they have a dilemma. We have been brainwashed into a nation of obsessive cleaners, so we demand the most effective products, and eco cleaners do not have a reputation for cleaning well. But in tests, EnvironCleaner cleaned as well as the leading players. This is a key point to remember in any marketing of ethical products (and which is highlighted in the section on the Ethical Sphere). The product's performance and the consumer benefit it delivers still remain a key selling point. Very few consumers will compromise just to have something that is a little more eco-friendly. If it doesn't clean well, or as well as the others, the product can make as many claims as it likes about saving the planet but after one purchase the eco-consumer will go back to tried and trusted brands.

In the case of EnvironCleaner, we decided to look at the advantages of a natural versus chemical cleaner. It seemed obvious that if the process of removing dirt and bacteria then left a skin of nasty chemicals behind, it was not leaving a home clean. I certainly wouldn't want to eat a sandwich laid on a surface covered in chemicals.

Looking at different audiences, it appeared that the older group were more inclined to buy eco-ethical products but the bigger market was mums, especially those with small children and babies. A mother puts the health of the kids top of the list; after all, that's why they buy all these chemicals – a clean home is a safe home. Well, not when you know the truth.

Mothers are also well networked and word of mouth is a naturally powerful marketing tool. Research I saw on Pampers revealed that word of mouth was one of the most powerful influencers upon mothers to buy Pampers. People trust people more than advertising.

REFRAMING FROM THE ENVIRONMENT TO THE HOME ENVIRONMENT

So the repositioning we took was from 'the environmental' to the 'home environment'. We wanted to redefine what 'clean' meant, defining it as 'dirt, germ and chemical free'. A very powerful positioning, especially as it's both a rational and emotional pitch.

Too many green brands think that all you need is a green badge, or to use clichéd green words or images; that there's a green consumer just waiting to buy. Maybe that's why many green products don't have sizeable slices of the market.

However, even green consumers have options and will make compromises. Like any product selling into any market you need to do your research – get great consumer insight, select the right audience and position the product correctly. Good marketing can sell a product to a much wider audience than just green shoppers. Good marketing is an investment, not a cost, and I would recommend any investor that was looking to back a green brand to make sure they are investing enough in consumer insight, strategy and great marketing. Without it, the brand may grow organically but it'll be slow and when another recession comes along, it gets delisted.

GREEN ENLIGHTENMENT OR JUMPING ON THE GREEN BANDWAGON?

Clorox, associated with household bleach in the US, has decided to become a leading light in the green marketplace. This is quite a change of direction and doesn't sit comfortably with its nasty chemical products. Is this a case of environmental enlightenment or just jumping on a bandwagon to make a buck? Either way, they're offering the consumer a green choice. Green purists will be appalled but if the green market becomes stronger than the chemical one, sooner or later every cleaner will be greener.

Clorox are well aware that this is a growing marketplace and with a strong distribution network and deals with Wal-Mart and Safeway they are better placed to mass produce and mass distribute a natural cleaner. This is the power big brands can use in order to make a greater difference. Sure, there are many small eco-cleaners out there but they are powerless, with little influence and can't meet the supply and logistical demands of the big super-markets. Sorry, but you're not going to change the world from a corner shop.

The rather bluntly and unimaginatively named Green Works (Clorox's first new brand in 20 years) comprises a range of five cleaning products (which includes glass, toilet and bathroom specific cleaners). The marketing literature claims Green Works to be 'at least 99 percent natural'. The products are made from coconuts and lemon oil, formulated to be biodegradable and non-allergenic, are packaged in recyclable bottles and are not tested on animals.

As part of the marketing launch, they managed to get the Sierra Club to endorse the product (Sierra Club may mean nothing in the UK but it carries influence in the States). Many greens feel that as Clorox is responsible for millions of gallons of chlorine passing through our homes and into the environment, the fact the Sierra Club is endorsing this product is wrong.

SUMMARY

Having discovered just how terrible chemical cleaners are I now buy ethical ones. Once consumers discover the truth they do too. For years we've been sold lies about germs and been conned into thinking that things are clean when they aren't because a film of chemicals on your kitchen table isn't clean. Even though the chemical companies have big pockets I really do believe that the writing's on the wall. The opportunity for natural eco-ethical cleaners is gigantic, though hardly any have good marketing and their packaging is terrible. As with eggs, we now buy free range as our first choice, so eco-cleaners will become first choice also.

25
GREEN INSURANCE
AND FINANCE

SLOW TURNING WHEELS – WHERE ARE ALL THE ECO BRANDS?

Why has the insurance industry, especially the automotive field, been so slow to go green big time? In fact, there's very little outside the automotive field. There are a few small number of eco players in the market such as ibuyeco, Green Insurance, Climate Sure and ETA. Bigger players include More Than with Green Wheels and of course, the most credible name in ethical finance, the Co-op. Even though brands like More Than have had a green version since 2006 and the Co-op longer, the insurance business hasn't been able to make a big splash with green insurance. This could be because they lack credibility. After all, the main driving ethos of any financial institute is money, which doesn't make you feel like they really care about the environment or people. But I suspect it's really because of the approach they take, which is over cautious and underfunded. They have tested it badly and rejected it. I was told that Elephant failed to sell green polices and I know of a few other insurance companies who have experimented and failed. There's a great opportunity for those who see it but it takes trial and error and an understanding that knowledge of consumer attitudes is the key to success. It's not enough to just think in generic 'green' terms, that kind of shallow thinking isn't good business thinking: 'Just because something doesn't do what you planned it to do in the first place doesn't mean it's useless ... the genius is the person who sees an opportunity where others see failure'. Such is the wisdom of Thomas Edison, inventor.

IS THE CUSTOMER SAVING THE PLANET OR JUST SAVING MONEY?

Insurance has become even more of a cut price, cut throat business during the recession. Many believe that it's all about price and even brand is making little difference. The primary proposition and search criterion is low price. Every company claims to give you a lower price than your current company.

And it's here that the opportunity to sell green or ethical insurance lies. When a market is reduced to its lowest level – price – it has no lower point to go. In this market 'value brands' start to emerge, ones that are smarter and more innovative. They offer the consumer better value by adding values to their proposition. Ethics is a great value to add. It offers a brand a differential but most of all it offers a platform from which to engage consumers emotionally.

The phrase 'car insurance' is the most highly valued Google AdWord, and any search reveals a vast number of players in the market, with many intermediaries offering to make the process of selection simpler. It's also spurred the growth of names that are just micro brands that skin bigger operators. The web allows insurance companies and brokers to experiment with new products and alternative brands, without spending a fortune on traditional TV ads.

One green brand, Climatesure, is actually making this saving a feature of its sell, by telling consumers that what it doesn't spend on ads it uses to cut costs and fund sustainable energy projects and carbon offset projects around the world. And as the industry believes that green drivers are better drivers, they will claim less, yet another saving. You get great value without having to pay extra to offset your guilt. They even feature pie charts (though badly drawn ones) on the website. It's an emotionally appealing piece of rational thinking. However, I think the claim to be the first to offer green insurance may be a bit debatable.

Climatesure are also extending into travel, home and other areas. Their marketing strategy seems to be web and PR based, hoping that word of mouth will spread the word. They have appeared on Passion for the Planet radio (a brilliant digital radio station dedicated to health, ethics and the environment) but without a major push to get consumers onto the website, growth could be slow. However, their site is certainly one of the most compelling.

eGreen Insurance (a broker) has partnered up with the World Land Trust and uses £25 of each policy to buy a half acre plot of land in the rainforest. This they claim will save the rainforest and help offset your car's CO_2, though the latter fact seems a token as the trees are there anyway. I don't feel that they have really pushed this far enough, it's all a bit factual and unemotional.

ETA (the Environmental Transport Association) offers both insurance that offsets your CO_2 and breakdown cover. They even offer a route finder that gives you the greenest route for your journey by calculating the amount of CO_2 you'll produce and the opportunity to offset it. London to

Sheffield produces 52 kg (or 26 500 litres) of CO2, for example. It's a great tool for engaging customers. The challenge for the insurance industry has always been trying to hit people just before they renew and this tool is a brilliant way to draw the customer in so as to become familiar with the brand. Engagement in a brand is so important if you want to build trust. Once people trust you, they'll buy you.

IBUYECO – DOING YOUR BIT THROUGH INSURANCE

Ibuyeco, launched in May 2007, sells itself on being 100% carbon neutral car insurance. It highlights that transport is responsible for 25% of CO2 emissions; this may be true but that's not all cars, for me that's a bit of spin. They are in effect a broker and part of the Budget Group, an insurance intermediary, but they do deliver cheap and highly competitive insurance. The idea was dreamt up at a senior management conference in Marakesh, following a 'Dragon's Den' style exercise. BGL Group is the UK's largest privately owned personal lines insurance intermediary and works with brands like the Post Office and M&S.

Using TGI data they identified over 2.4 million deep greens and almost 8 million light greens – that's a big market. Unlike Climatesure, Ibuyeco launched with an integrated media mix using DRTV, online media and direct mail.

Ibuyeco's success probably isn't just down to its environmental spin but also because it does offer highly competitive prices. They've targeted green consumers well but the growth has to be in the larger population. By teaming up with the Carbon Neutral Company they offer the customer, for a small fee, the chance to offset their car's carbon – so they can 'do their bit'.

Their website has some useful links, a fun area, a guide to greener motoring and a live online survey. According to their visitors, 71% of people believe that they can make a difference to climate change. They've spotted the enormous potential of the caravanning market and have also linked up with third parties. Through the Country Music Festival they're offering people the chance to offset their journey. Their TV ad is a bit cheesy and probably good at raising brand awareness but the proposition is too generic. Offsetting is a good approach but somehow not engaging enough on TV. However, to date they have exceeded their targets for growth although they found that a fair percentage of customers were not classified as traditional greens (probably the ones who bought cheap). They've also offset more than 100 tonnes of carbon. No bad at all.

Their website is also full of advice on reducing a car's 'carbon tyre print'. The customer gets cheap insurance (rational) combined with a sense of 'doing my bit' (emotional). The same insurance could work probably just as well with a humanitarian offer or any other green offer because it's an emotional benefit and few insurance companies offer any. I don't wish to imply that the insurance market doesn't get it, but because their culture is very rational, logical, linear and retail, emotions don't come into it. It's all about the money. If that was the case then the only brand left in the marketplace would be the cheapest, yet it's full of dozens of brands, many not really brands at all. In a market where the only difference is price – this is what happens when markets reach the lowest common denominator – then of course you can argue that the consumer selects rationally. However, the consumer is not a rational animal by nature. Give them an emotional reason to buy (and many insurance quotes are much of a muchness these days) and you stand a chance of winning a bigger slice of the market. That's what FMCG brands do.

Adding ethics to the proposition at no extra cost has to be a winner. That's not to say that any other emotional addition or promotional offer couldn't be just as effective. But in an environment when the environment is both high-lighted and fashionable and relevant to motoring, a green benefit is a good marketing move. No surprise then, that Ibuyeco has done well in its first year and hit its targets. There will no doubt be many followers. When I worked with More Than insurance I proposed a green product; it fitted well with their colour (green) and their audience (mainly older people with values). More Than were in a prime position to market green car insurance and have a great customer base to work on. Since then they have ventured into the market with Green Wheels, though not through the team we worked with, so I can't take any credit. Sadly, it seems to be a product they don't promote very hard, even on their website. A great shame because if they put some serious budget and good creative work behind it I believe it could be a winner.

THE NEW WORLD OF MICRO BRANDING

When you go to internet insurance aggregator sites (as half of car insurance buyers do) such as Moneysupermarket. com, Comparethemarket.com or U-Switch, the only representation of brands are small logos, often no bigger than 1 cm × 2 cm. Brands exist as thumbnails so they have to get their message and brand values across quickly and power-fully. Decisions are being made largely on price but even so, consumers have to filter, so spontaneous decisions have to be made. This has created a new industry in analytics, people who try to develop a science behind the use of words and icons (or brand logos). Although Google won't let you put an instruction like 'click' into your copy, some brands have discovered tagging the end of their url, http://www.greengnomeinsurance.com/click, has increased response rates. I'd advise experimenting with elements such as this but be wary of creating rules.

Understanding what works and what doesn't is good marketing practice but it's important to separate observation, learnings and trends from rules. To stand as a rule, it has to create the same behaviour each time and be predictable, so you need to understand all the dynamics behind it. Science is very exact about what a rule is; it uses the term 'theory' for the unproven and in marketing there really are no rules, just theories.

Data and statistics are powerful and essential things but there is one saying that everyone should have printed above a data spread sheet: 'Don't make the measurable important – make the important measurable'.

Numbers can lead to bad marketing practice – a rigid set of rules and false assumptions – we all know what happens when you give a politician statistics. Marketing is an art backed by science, not a science with art tagged on. There really is little certainty in the world, people are all very different and with so much change and so many variables it would be dangerous to write a rule book, however in our basic need for certainty we inevitably do. A rule book is a great fall back; we can protect our arses and use it to defer responsibility. But great marketing is about taking risks, standing at the edge and redefining the landscape. And if you aren't someone else will.

The direct marketing industry restricted itself for many years by using rules and statistics, rather than instinct. A great saying often quoted in the industry is, 'some people use statistics like a drunk uses a lamp post, for support not illumination'. I also like 'If you use rules as a crutch you won't get very far before you fall over'. Use rules as guidelines (not tramlines) or as something to break.

The myth that an envelope line makes people open a letter more than one without was never true and has never been substantiated in any campaign I've worked on. But many people believe it. In fact, in one research group we conducted for SKY, consumers were more inclined to bin it without opening it. Why? Because, as one consumer put it, 'if it's got a line on you know its junk mail so it's safe to bin'.

WHAT INSURANCE CAN LEARN FROM SELLING SHOES

If you tap in 'Green Car Insurance' there are few players. So is this a sign of a great opportunity or that there just isn't a market? This brings to mind a great marketing story about a father who owned a shoe company. He was soon to retire but knew his two sons couldn't run the company together as they never agreed on anything. He decided that just one would take over the business, but which one? After much thought, he decided to set them a test. He sent them both to Tibet to look at setting up a shoe shop. After a month both sons returned. The first reported that after weeks of travelling, he was depressed because no one wore shoes, just straw sandals: 'There's no market there father'. The second son saw it differently. 'I travelled for weeks in amazement', he said excitedly. 'Everyone wears sandals, they haven't discovered real shoes yet, the potential is amazing'. The second son got the company. I think the first became a monk.

ONCE BITTEN, TWICE SHY

It's easy not to see potential or to miss it because we tried and failed. Too many brands try once and write it off. Marketing is always about exploring and experimenting. One client I met at a conference said to me, 'I tried creativity once, it didn't work'. My reply was, 'I tried a scratch card once and didn't win a thing. The third time I won £150'.

My own feelings are that many companies have just flirted with the eco-ethical market, with little or no professional advice or understanding of the eco-ethical consumer. They just tried to do a low budget DIY stab at the market. No surprise then that they failed. I can see why many test campaigns fail. Or alternatively, they seek advice in the wrong place, using their traditional advertising, PR, digital, design or direct marketing agency who may be excellent at traditional marketing but think all you need to do to reach green people is use the words 'green' or 'environmental'. Sorry to have a go at agencies but there's a reason why there are specialists in the market. Look them up on Ethical Junction, there's a wide range of marketing, advertising, design, digital and PR agencies who are members.

There are many avenues to explore (see the section on the Ethical Sphere) but try these:

- An environmental insurance that offers an offset.
- An environmental insurance that supports a key rainforest protection and development project.
- An ethical insurance that supports transport in order to help charities in developing worlds, i.e. helping kids get to school so they can learn.
- An ethical insurance that helps support a campaign to encourage people to use cars less, i.e. supports the Walk to School campaign.
- An ethical insurance that supports any animal charity because we give more to animals than people (and we give more to people charities than to environmental ones).

But beware of the words you use. Just throwing in words like 'green', 'environmental' or 'ethical' can sound like greenwash. Focus on the cause and ask the simple question 'what's in it emotionally for the consumer?'

CAUTION AND UNCERTAINTY

Thomas Edison made a simple but powerful observation, 'Fear creates failure, courage creates success'.

Having worked with a wide range of financial service companies, being brave is not high on the agenda. Since 9/11 risk management has been replaced by risk aversion, I recommend that everyone reads 'The Culture of Fear' by Frank Furedi. It outlines how as a society we have stopped taking risks and how, as a consequence, we are not progressing.

Taking risks goes hand in hand with growth and entrepreneurialism. But it scares the willies out of most people in finance. I don't wish to be harsh but most marketing people I meet are deeply frustrated by this cautious culture.

I used to work with NatWest. They failed to win the hearts and minds of the customer in the 1990s because they were cold, rational, very boring and wouldn't take risks (very linear). They failed to connect with the customer and most of the work was dull. While they were trying to be a little nice in ads their managers were writing vicious, aggressive letters to overdrawn customers. Your marketing is only as strong as the weakest link to the customer. It was frightening how their ethos, or lack of one, was damaging their communications.

I recall one presentation to NatWest, we'd come up with six great ideas that were fun, engaging and communicated the message really well. Their initial reaction was great, a real WOW! factor. They looked pleased. But then there was a turning point, the point at which I think a marketing manager suddenly remembers it's not him that's buying the work but his employer. Emotional positivity soon declined into rational negativity. The WOW! factor was replaced with the 'what if' factor. Finally, the end comment was, 'sorry, we can't run these ideas, as brilliant as they are, we're a bank'. I'm not sure who was more disappointed, us or the client. It must be like being a monk in a good bar, you want to have fun but your religion doesn't allow you to.

Psychologists will tell you that we need security and therefore certainty. Experimentation and creativity require you to go to a place outside your comfort zone, a place that the culture of many businesses find hard to enter. They need certainty so they can only go to the edges. Challenger brands and dynamic companies like Nike, Apple and many technology companies have a culture of challenge, change and creativity, which allows them to go beyond the conventional and explore new markets and ideas. But new consumer attitudes and new trends lead us into the unknown, so naturally we are cautious, especially if we are measured more on our failures than successes. If just one insurance company adopted Nike's philosophy, they'd dominate the market. When MTV first started out they used failure not as a bad measure but as one designed to prove innovation. The more risks people took, the more failures there'd be. By building in failure as part of the journey you allow people to push the boundaries, people need permission to fail.

FORGET GREEN, TRY ETHICS

As I've said, selling green insurance is not as simple as just offering green insurance. You may well trust your existing company but do you feel you are being sold a token policy or do you feel the company really cares? With so much greenwash and corporate environmental tokenism about it's no wonder the consumer is cynical. A new name, small, fresh and seemingly passionate about the environment would appear more credible. When you hear that someone like Ibuyeco has launched in order to help motorists offset their CO2 and be more environmentally friendly it sounds more genuine. The fact that they are a division of a very large insurance company and that the product is largely a skin isn't apparent to the customer. It's a good way to do it.

Alternatively, a trusted name with ethical values can be a good place to offer insurance. The National Trust and RSPB both have a branded electricity policy, for example, so why not insurance? If Greenpeace tried to sell you green insurance you'd worry about their capability to cover you, but if backed by Norwich Union you might think differently. Greenpeace offers you trust and sincerity, Norwich Union credibility and capability. There will always be those drivers who like it as an idea, it fits their inner green beliefs, but persuading the masses – and that's where the money is – is a different game. People need to believe you can deliver cover and that you care.

Beside the deeper green's who will seek it out, I think there are three key groups (you could easily define many more) to consider. This is speculative because every company would need to consider all their variable factors before they could do this exercise. However, it serves as an example. I'm a great believer in creating your own grouping systems and not relying on others because with that comes assumptions.

The 'nice to have' like the warm feeling of a greener policy, knowing they are offsetting their carbon tyre print. They feel less guilty and more responsible. It's a good thing to do and these people like to notch up good deeds. It's an inner driven act. They are more than likely to respond to key words and may even search for environmentally positive insurance, but they are not deep green.

The 'look at me aren't I green' types use green as a validation of their ethical credentials (which relate to their status). In short, they are keeping up with the green Joneses.

These people are outwardly driven and would like to have a big sticker on their window to tell everyone they have green insurance. They are also the type who would be most likely to get involved with a friend get friend campaign. Recommending it to others allows them a platform to tell others how ethical they are.

The third group are best described as 'rationally indifferent'. They wouldn't disagree that we should all be taking responsibility. In street surveys they create the gap between intent and actual action. When surveyed they'll tick the boxes but their actions don't follow. They see insurance and many financial policies as a function, a 'must have', so it's all about price and convenience. Keep it simple, keep it cheap and quick. It's insurance, it won't save the world and the idea of paying any extra is a no go. They may be cynical and think carbon neutral companies are just paying a devil's tax in order to appear innocent and that carbon offsetting is a scam. They may even argue that while big industry in China and India are destroying the planet what difference will car insurance make?

THE GREEN WALL

To grab this group you need to engage with them emotionally (not something I think many financial companies are good at). Ironically, selling them insurance that helps people in the Third World could be more effective than saving the environment. For a start, it's different. The human need to connect means that we relate to people far more than trees. If your car insurance costs the same but supports transport projects to help kids in Africa get to school so they can get an education, many drivers may well think differently. It also gets past the 'green wall' as I call it, the consumer reaction against being told all the time they have to be green to be good. It's like kids who are told not to drink, do drugs or have sex, after a while they create a barrier of indifference to the messages, something I've seen working in the sexual health field. We all now know carbon offsetting is a very dubious way to save the planet, a sticking plaster solution to climate change. But helping kids get schooling, now that's tangible. It feels real and as a consumer I can relate to it. Suddenly my car insurance isn't just insurance; it's ensuring that others get a better life. Sign me up.

This is one way you can think outside the green box and explore other more emotional offerings. There's a difference between feeling 'I'm making a positive contribution and creating change for the better', and feeling that 'if I don't do my bit I should feel guilty', or worse, 'I'm a sinner'. This has been one of the problems surrounding the whole environmentalism issue in the media and the government's approach. We all feel we are being chastised, made to feel guilty ('you must do your bit') and made to feel responsible as if we are bad people. Yet most of us feel that it's governments and big businesses who really should take responsibility, they led us down this road.

GREEN CAR INSURANCE, A CONSUMER EXPERIENCE

Looking for green car insurance, three companies came up: eGreen ('eGreen insurance will help reduce your car insurance costs and your CO2 emissions, take a more ethical approach to your car insurance and help tackle …'); Ibuyeco ('Get Cheap Car Insurance Quotes and help save the planet'); and the Green Insurance Company ('Free Carbon Offset on all Car Insurance policies. Get a quote now'). However, another site linked me to More Than.

The link to More Than Green Wheel insurance just took me to the homepage rather than a dedicated green insurance site – a big mistake. I tried going through the Together site, same problem. It's a simple fact but if I am after green car insurance I don't want to be on the general car insurance page. It makes More Than's claims feel token. What More Than should have done is set up a dedicated green insurance site offering car, caravan, home and personal green cover. It's all very well having the CEO of Royal & Sun Alliance (More Than's parent company) say they are dedicated to giving their customers 'the opportunity to take responsibility for their carbon "tyre-print"', but it didn't feel like that. If they are really dedicated, then they could do more with the site. However, when you do visit the Green Wheel zone, it's very helpful with tips on better driving (as can be found on the government's Act on CO2 site) and information (More Than were the first insurance company invited to join the Together campaign). They also introduce a novel idea, a Green Box that monitors your car's eco performance. To buy green insurance I had to go back to the main home page where there appeared to be no green zone.

Ibuyeco was a far better and friendlier site and managed to bring cost saving and planet values together in a positive way without cheesy clichés. It's a well designed site.

The Green Insurance Company has opted for a strange looking green monster and a clichéd headline, which is very outdated and cheesy: SAVE MORE THAN JUST MONEY ON YOUR CAR INSURANCE – HELP SAVE THE ENVIRONMENT AT NO EXTRA COST. Factually, 100% off-setting of a car's emissions is not saving the environment. The green monster does have a personality and gives the brand a stronger visual look. The greener car driver is rewarded with a better rate and they do donate 5% of profits to charity, though I have no idea which one. I always recommend that if you want to make a feature of your charity support, tell customers who and how you support them and put a link on your website. It's simple but so few brands think about it.

WHEN THE LEFT HAND DOESN'T KNOW WHAT THE RIGHT HAND'S DOING

Looking around various websites there seems to be a lack of connection between one element and another. It seems not everyone is getting the idea that the company has an ethical message to deliver. Why doesn't The Green Insurance Company have a section on their website about their environmental policies or of what charities they are supporting?

One of the biggest blunders I've come across are HSBC's banner ads selling greener loans but featuring a very un-eco looking 4 × 4. This is the classic problem when not everyone in the team gets it. For the banner designer it was probably just another job, any car will do and like most things on the web, done quick and cheap. That's not their only blunder. HSBC also printed hundreds of thousands of multi-page leaflets for their Green Sale that started with the line 'we are dedicated to reducing paper wastage'.

Given the vast and diverse channels most brands are using it's important to make sure you are checking every element. You are only as strong as your weakest link and if you mess up on your website, no matter how perfect the ads are, this is the one thing that can be your undoing.

This problem can be even worse in large corporations when one department is saying something very different from another. The case of Shell promoting F1 racing in one campaign and trying to push the environment in another was a classic clash.

With ethical campaigns it's very important that CSR and marketing departments work together and that CSR is allowed input, after all, they'll spot a greenwash campaign or flaws in the copy before you run it. And if you do get 'The Guardian' trying to pull you apart they are the ones best able to justify your claims. It's very easy for marketing, and especially advertising agencies, to slip into sales think and overlook the consequences of their ads.

SUMMARY

The insurance industry hasn't been quick to venture into green marketing and hasn't even touched ethical issues. Many would say this is due to a cautious attitude. But it could be because they are all too busy trying to undercut each other.

Insurance ads are rarely inspired and Esure's campaign was voted one of the worst of all time. They defended their bad ads by the uptake in policies but if they'd done decent work they'd have sold even more. There are plenty of brands who can give you a case study about how better ads sell more than bad ones.

There's a growing opportunity for insurance brands to grab a market share but they'll need to get it right. And to do that they'll need to take risks and approach the consumer with understanding rather than thinking like market traders – pile it high, sell it cheap.

26
BONUS CHAPTERS
AND WEBSITE

It seems to me that we can learn something from other areas of publishing, in this case films. During the writing of this book there were a number of chapters that we took out, some because the original manuscript was 30 000 words too long (there's over 63 000 words in this book). There were also many areas and brands that we could have written about, in the case of the Co-op a whole book.

Ambitiously, we plan to have a section where brands, big or small, can freely download their own case studies. This will provide a useful resource for those studying eco-ethical marketing. Ideally, we want it to become a hub for ethical marketing information and ideas.

I hope that this book has been an interesting read, not just a factual one. I do find many marketing books dry and dull. If we have made any mistakes or you feel you've been misrepresented please contact us via the site and we'll be happy to publish any corrections. We have made every effort to get the facts correct but sometimes sources can be inaccurate and some companies just haven't responded to our request to verify data.

If you want to update figures or add new data we'll have a section for that as well on the site.

This is a live issue and any book remains a fixed moment in time while the website will allow everyone to keep up with the present.

There's also a dedicated Facebook group – Ethical Marketing & The New Consumer.

If you want to book me for lectures or workshops on ethical marketing (or creativity), you'll also find details of my agents on the site too. My consultancy, Symple, is also available for giving advice on ethical marketing. Visit the agency site, http://www.symple.co.uk.

CREATIVE ORCHESTRA

Since writing this book, and as we go to print, I've just launched a unique ethically driven venture called Creative Orchestra (http://www.creativeorchestra.com). It's been set up to incubate young creative talent and find a value for that talent in the market place. We set up a proper creative department in amazing offices in Islington which house 25 of the best young talents working under experienced Creative Directors. At launch we had seven nationalities, a fascinating cultural mix. By default, we found that we've set up one of the first independent creative departments in the world (independent of an agency, the same route that media departments have taken) and also one of the top 20 in size. And it's all available to hire by brands or agencies looking for fresh ideas and new thinking. It's been set up as a Social Enterprise (CIC) so all the profits go back to the creatives that work there. I'll also be posting updates on this venture on the site.

My final point is that if anyone asks you to write a book remember it takes three times longer than you ever imagined – Wiley were very tolerant. My advice is to go away and find somewhere quiet (I went to Spain) and get a good researcher. I was lucky to have Sarah Eden who did a lot of the research and analysis of press cuttings. She knows her stuff in the eco-ethical field and also did the first round of editing. A goldmine! Thanks Sarah.

Having written this I plan to write three more books, with much fewer words, however. 'THUNK' (a different way to think) is a follow on to Paul Arden's two books on creativity. 'How to Think Like A Dyslexic' is a similar book but in support of the dyslexia charity Xtraordinary People. And 'DUMPED' is a collection of images of objects that have been dumped in the street – fridges, TVs, ironing boards, chairs, etc. This one will be dedicated to an environmental charity.

INDEX

*Index compiled by Annette
   Musker*